THE LIVE-ACTION ANIMATED FILM

QUICK TAKES: MOVIES AND POPULAR CULTURE

Quick Takes: Movies and Popular Culture is a series offering suc-
cinct overviews and high-quality writing on cutting-edge themes
and issues in film studies. Authors offer both fresh perspectives
on new areas of inquiry and original takes on established topics.

SERIES EDITORS:

Gwendolyn Audrey Foster is Willa Cather Professor Emerita of
Film Studies at the University of Nebraska, Lincoln. She is an
award-winning experimental filmmaker and a prolific author.

Wheeler Winston Dixon is the James Ryan Professor Emeritus
of Film Studies at the University of Nebraska, Lincoln. He is the
author of many books, including *A Short History of Film*, 3rd edi-
tion, and an internationally known experimental filmmaker.

Christina N. Baker,
*Black Women
Directors*

Rebecca
Bell-Metereau,
Transgender Cinema

Blair Davis,
Comic Book Movies

Jonna Eagle,
War Games

Carmelo Esterrich,
Star Wars Multiverse

Lester D. Freidman,
Sports Movies

Desirée J. Garcia,
The Movie Musical

Steven Gerrard,
*The Modern British
Horror Film*

Barry Keith Grant,
Monster Cinema

Julie Grossman,
The Femme Fatale

Daniel Herbert,
*Film Remakes and
Franchises*

Kyle Meikle,
*The Live-Action
Animated Film*

Ian Olney,
Zombie Cinema

Valérie K. Orlando,
New African Cinema

Carl Platinga,
Alternative Realities

Stephen Prince,
Apocalypse Cinema

Stephen Prince,
Digital Cinema

Dahlia Schweitzer,
Haunted Homes

Dahlia Schweitzer,
L.A. Private Eyes

Steven Shaviro,
Digital Music Videos

David Sterritt,
Rock 'n' Roll Movies

John Wills,
Disney Culture

The Live-Action Animated Film

KYLE MEIKLE

RUTGERS UNIVERSITY PRESS

New Brunswick, Camden, and Newark, New Jersey
London and Oxford

Rutgers University Press is a department of Rutgers, The State University
of New Jersey, one of the leading public research universities in the nation.
By publishing worldwide, it furthers the University's mission of dedication
to excellence in teaching, scholarship, research, and clinical care.

Library of Congress Cataloging-in-Publication Data
Names: Meikle, Kyle author
Title: The live-action animated film / Kyle Meikle.
Description: New Brunswick : Rutgers University Press, [2025] |
Series: Quick takes : movies and popular culture |
Includes bibliographical references and index.
Identifiers: LCCN 2025017746 | ISBN 9781978828612 paperback |
ISBN 9781978828629 hardback
Subjects: LCSH: Animated films—History and criticism | Animation
(Cinematography) | Cinematography—Special effects
Classification: LCC NC1765 .M395 2025
LC record available at https://lccn.loc.gov/2025017746

A British Cataloging-in-Publication record for this book is available
from the British Library.

References to internet websites (URLs) were accurate at the time of
writing. Neither the author nor Rutgers University Press is responsible for
URLs that may have expired or changed since the manuscript was prepared.

∞ The paper used in this publication meets the requirements of the
American National Standard for Information Sciences—Permanence of
Paper for Printed Library Materials, ANSI Z39.48-1992.

rutgersuniversitypress.org

CONTENTS

THE LIVE-ACTION ANIMATED FILM

INTRODUCTION

Robert Zemeckis's *Who Framed Roger Rabbit* (1988) takes place in 1947 Los Angeles, where (in the words of the film's press kit) "famous actors and actresses direct from their posh homes in Beverly Hills and Bel Air" mingle with "Toons, the colorful stars and superstars of cartoons who commute from Toontown, the suburb of Hollywood where down is up, up is down, and anything goes" (Touchstone Pictures 12). On the fictional Maroon Studios' backlot, live-action stars, script girls, grips, and instrumentalists mix with all manner of animated wildlife, including a haughty ostrich, a top-hatted frog, a tutued hippo, some magic brooms (from 1940's *Fantasia*), a stork delivering mail, and a group of preening bovines in a literal cattle call. Down really is up: In a thudding lunch break, the hippo sends one hapless stagehand airborne with his sandwich in hand when she settles next to him on a bench. The Toons commute their animatedness to the live-action world around them.

Roger Rabbit's wayward La La Land, where "Toons and humans exist side by side in the bustling movie community" (Touchstone Pictures), stemmed from real-world precedent. A year (in reality) before *Roger Rabbit*'s fictional case unfolds, the director Nick Grinde mused, in a 1946 issue of *The Screen Writer*, on the past and future of the "part flesh and part ink talking picture" (19). By the time of Grinde's writing, live action had long livened animation, and animation had long livened live action. The tradition stretched at least as far back as the human fingers that reached beyond the fourth wall to bring a stick-figure clown to life in Émile Cohl's *Fantasmagorie* (1908)—in a trope so common that the scholar Donald Crafton coined the phrase "the hand of the artist" (the title of a stop-motion 1906 short) to describe it ("Animation Iconography"). In 1924's *Trip to Mars*, meanwhile, Ko-Ko the Clown (who appears headed into Maroon Studios during *Roger Rabbit*'s opening) spaces out in a rocket alongside his live-action creator, Max Fleischer. A decade on, animation lent a pep to the stop-motion step of the soldiers in Laurel and Hardy's *Babes in Toyland* (1934), on which Grinde himself served as cowriter. By the 1940s, then, the practice of combining live action with animation wasn't just standard but stale. In "Greasepaint, Inkwell & Co.," Grinde remarks that *The Three Caballeros*, released just two years prior, woke a dozy "Rip Van Winkle of the show business" that had "lay dormant" since Fleischer's, Walter Lantz's, and

Walt Disney's respective "bi-partisan" dalliances with Ko-Ko, Colonel Heeza Liar, and Little Alice in the 1920s and 1930s (19). He side-eyes those "astute prophets" who "predict[] a lethargic future for this renovated method of picture making," adding, "They could be wrong again, as they had been about the talking picture twenty years ago." But the mixed reception of Disney's latest mixed production doesn't bode well: "There is no doubt but that the galloping paintings mingle most convincingly with the live girls on the beach. But after a bravo for the achievement, there was a tendency to say 'So what?'" (19). Grinde suggests an assortment of stories better suited to "animaction": older hits—like *Babes* (which Disney would remake in the 1960s), Disney's *Snow White and the Seven Dwarfs* (1937), and Victor Fleming's *The Wizard of Oz* (1939)—that could be remade to further cleave "the real and the fantastic"; fantastic epics like *The Arabian Nights* and *The Odyssey*; children's stories like *The Water-Babies*, "Jack and the Beanstalk," *Alice in Wonderland*, "Cinderella," and *Winnie-the-Pooh*; and "up-to-the-minute pictures" involving "psychiatric problems, dream sequences," or "Heaven or Hell" (21–22). Only then, says Grinde, might the Rip Van Winkle of flesh and ink "come into its own and pave the way for a general release of stories of this type which so far have been more or less earthbound" (21).

That Rip Van Winkle did wake, fitfully, over the next half century, ambling and dancing along the paths that Grinde laid out. In the 1950s, one-off dream sequences mingling live action and animation distinguished up-to-the-minute musicals like *My Dream Is Yours* (1949), in which Doris Day and Jack Carson cut a rug with Bugs Bunny, and *Dangerous When Wet* (1953), in which Esther Williams synchronously swims with Tom Cat and Jerry Mouse. Gene Kelly, who himself tangoes with Jerry in 1945's *Anchors Aweigh*, blended live action with animation in an *Arabian Nights*–inspired segment of 1956's *Invitation to the Dance* and then again in 1967's made-for-TV *Jack and the Beanstalk*. Disney drew from children's literature in *Mary Poppins* (1964) and 1971's *Bedknobs and Broomsticks*, ostensibly live-action films that incorporate animation for just a musical number or two. And, around the same time, the special-effects maestro Ray Harryhausen mined all manner of Greek, Middle Eastern, and Roman mythology for the stop-motion creatures that populated *The 7th Voyage of Sinbad* (1958), *Jason and the Argonauts* (1963), and *Clash of the Titans* (1981) (Grinde himself had recommended "a disagreeable fellow named Cyclops" as an excellent subject for the blended technique [21].)

These intermittent experiments in combining animation with live action reached an apotheosis in the block-busting, chaotic *Roger Rabbit*, 1988's highest grossing film;

Beetlejuice, whose stop-motion sandworms and undulating sculptures owed much of their odd charm to Harryhausen's feature creatures (not the least *Jason*'s Hydra and *The Golden Voyage of Sinbad*'s [1973] murderous six-armed statue), came in at number ten. *Roger Rabbit* stretched the live-action animated interludes of yesteryear to greater length and greater success. As distantly as 2024, FranchiseRe's David Gross was still using *Roger Rabbit* as the "ground-breaker" benchmark for live-action animated films' success (measuring it against and alongside titles like *IF* [2024], *Alvin and the Chipmunks* [2007], *Sonic the Hedgehog* [2020], *Paddington* [2014], and *Peter Rabbit* [2018]); he estimated its adjusted haul at a cool $1 billion.

Following *Roger Rabbit*'s apogee, mixed pictures began to dominate Hollywood. But those pictures looked slightly different from the live-action animated efforts of the 1950s, 1960s, and 1970s. While the 1990s and early 2000s yielded several offbeat approximations of *Roger Rabbit* (*Cool World* [1992], *Evil Toons* [1992], *The Pagemaster* [1994], *Osmosis Jones* [2001], *Space Jam* [1996], and *Looney Tunes: Back in Action* [2003]), stop-motion combinations retreated mostly to the arthouse (*Faust* [1994], *Conspirators of Pleasure* [1996], *Monkeybone* [2001], and *The Life Aquatic with Steve Zissou* [2004]). Those films' combinations of live action and hand-drawn or hand-sculpted animation paled in comparison to the cutting-edge computer-generated (CG) imagery on the rise at multiplexes. *Roger*'s 2D rabbit and *Beetlejuice*'s latex sandworms gave way, bit by byte, to the fantastic digital costars of 1991's *Terminator 2: Judgment Day*, 1993's *Jurassic Park* (indebted to Harryhausen), 1995's *Casper*, and 1999's *Star Wars: Episode I—The Phantom Menace*, just as *Roger*'s Toontown and *Beetlejuice*'s Neitherworld ceded to digital realms like *What Dreams May Come*'s (1998) painterly heaven and hell—Grinde, prophetic again— and *The Matrix*'s (1999) matrix. Just a decade after *Roger Rabbit*'s and *Beetlejuice*'s box office success, half of 1998's ten highest grossing films included live-action affairs that made more or less extensive use of computer animation, whether *Armageddon*'s giant asteroid, *Godzilla*'s lizard king, *Saving Private Ryan*'s bullets, *Doctor Doolittle*'s chattering animals, or *The Truman Show*'s endless suburban sprawl. Just a decade later, in 2008, the only films in the top ten that *didn't* combine live action and animation were those that were fully CG in the first place, like *Kung Fu Panda* and *Madagascar: Escape 2 Africa*. The digital animation underpinning *The Dark Knight* and *Indiana Jones and the Kingdom of the Crystal Skull* (the top two titles) was standard and stale—animating supervillains and extraterrestrials, sure, but also more pedestrian matter like debris and trees.

In 1946, Grinde had envisioned a future where mixing live action and animation wouldn't be fitful but everyday, where "the infiltration of cartoon technique will not be called to your attention any more than the countryside outside of Spencer Tracy's train window is advertised as a trick" (26). By the first decade of the twenty-first century, that future had arrived. Grinde speculated that, eventually, "to announce 'part cartoon and part flesh' would be as unnecessary to a film with a legitimate story appeal as a listing of Betty Grable's chemical ingredients, intriguing as they might be" (26). The writer/director couldn't anticipate, perhaps, that animation would even be used to synthesize those intriguing ingredients, with computers providing Dakota Johnson's pubic hair in 2015's *Fifty Shades of Grey* and removing Henry Cavill's real-life mustache in 2017's *Justice League*. Just a couple of decades after *Roger Rabbit*, the line between live action and animation had become blurry enough for the Pixar mainstay Andrew Stanton to speculate that "with each proceeding year, it's going to be tougher to say what's an animated movie and what's not an animated movie" (Ball). The director himself blurred that line in his postapocalyptic heart warmer *WALL-E* (2008's eighth highest grossing film). The mostly computer-animated *WALL-E* not only features live-action inserts of Fred Willard (as the disgraced Buy n Large CEO Shelby Forthright) and several clips from 1969's *Hello, Dolly!* (the titular trash compactor's favorite film) but also a midfilm gag in which Stanton pans along a series of captains' portraits, progressing from strictly live action to more cartoonish faces. In this pan, live action *becomes* animation—gradually and near imperceptibly, in contrast to *Roger Rabbit*'s or *Looney Tunes: Back in Action*'s abrupt third-act reveals that characters we *thought* were live action are *actually* duplicitous toons in disguise. Stanton followed his own lead in 2012's *John Carter*, a live-action film that reportedly contained *more* character animations than the CG *WALL-E* (Brodesser-Akner).

The chapters that follow offer their own pan: from the middle of the twentieth century, when Grinde was writing (and when Roger Rabbit got framed) to the middle of the twenty-first, the setting of Steven Spielberg's 2018 fantasia *Ready Player One*, whose live-action animated mash-up led one YouTuber to ask if the film was "the New Roger Rabbit" (NowThis Nerd). Contemporary Hollywood blockbusters like *Ready Player One* can largely be understood as the end result of a century's worth of live-action animated tinkering, from some freewheeling stirrings in the 1910s, 1920s, and 1930s to sporadic cameos in the 1940s, 1950s, 1960s, and 1970s to a multiplexed ascent in the 1980s, 1990s, and beyond. We can trace a winding line from the artist's hand in *Fantasmagorie* to the computer-animated fingers that snap half of life out of existence in the Russo brothers' *Avengers: Infinity War* (2018). In the intervening years, dozens of animated characters—among them the title characters in *King Kong* (1933), *The Three Caballeros*, *Pete's Dragon* (1977), *Casper*, *Stuart Little* (1999), and *Ted* (2012)—crossed over into live-action worlds, or else live actors have crossed into theirs: the black-and-white Wonderland of the Alice comedies (1924–27), the chalk-drawing diversion of *Mary Poppins*, Toontown, *Cool World*, *The Matrix*, or the violet valleys of planet Vormir, from 2019's *Avengers: Endgame*. Viewed up close, live-action animated films (especially those of the pre-CG variety) may look idiosyncratic, if not downright outré; the animators Frank Thomas and Ollie Johnston actually describe Disney's midcentury hybrid films, like *The Three Caballeros*, in terms of experimentation (qtd. in Telotte, *Animating Space* 143). But, in the long view, those twentieth-century experiments in mixing 2D and stop-motion animation with live action appear more like the foundations for the towering franchises of the twenty-first century—the Lord of the Rings, Harry Potter, the Marvel Cinematic Universe—in which animation collapses into live action. Tellingly, Hollywood reached back to the mixed pictures of yesteryear in forging this new accord, with *Clash of the Titans* (2010), *Wrath of the Titans* (2012), *Pete's Dragon* (2016), and *Mary*

Poppins Returns (2018) remaking or reworking their earlier stop-motion or 2D-animated combinations in CG. Disney went even further still, reimagining its old, strictly animated classics as newly hybrid productions, in, for instance, *Alice in Wonderland* (2010), *Cinderella* (2015), and *Pooh*-riff *Christopher Robin* (2018)—all titles that Grinde had suggested for "animaction" in the first place (Disney also followed Grinde's suggestion in revisiting, if not remaking, the Yellow Brick Road, in 2013's live-action/CG *Oz the Great and Powerful*). Universal, meanwhile, took a cue from its competitor, refashioning the fully CG *How to Train Your Dragon* (2011) as a live-action animated feature in 2025. In twenty-first-century Hollywood, most roads led from or to the hybrid film.

The media theorist Lev Manovich famously asserted that cinema, "born from animation, . . . pushed animation to its periphery, only in the end to become one particular case of animation" (9). Over the course of a century, the live-action animated film foregrounded this peripheral play—the often centrifugal, in the end centripetal dance between cinema and animation (frequently framed as an actual tango). The contemporary blockbuster stems from a hundred years of detonations weakening the wall between live action and animation, shaking audiences' sense of the separation between these seeming opposites. As Maureen Furniss (5) notes, even though audiences and critics tend to define live action against animation (and vice versa), the two terms aren't intrinsically opposed, even if their *tendencies* are; live action leans toward mimesis (reproducing "natural reality"), and animation leans toward abstraction (concepts and forms). Depending on their tendencies, then, live-action animated films can occupy any number of spaces between the extremes of mimesis and abstraction—so that, per Furniss, *The Three Caballeros* might sit in the middle of that continuum, with *Jurassic Park* just to its left (closer to natural reality). The live-action animated film's fluidity explains why, as early as Disney's mixed Alice comedies, Russell Merritt and J. B. Kaufman can identify any number of "live-action Hollywood conventions" (29), while J. P. Telotte registers an "impetus towards [a] realist aesthetic" in the same series ("Disney's Alice Comedies" 339). When Industrial Light and Magic ensconces Iron Man in digital armor one hundred years later, making the screen superhero a little less live-action and a little more real, the special-effects company is simply following suit.

In the pages ahead, I suggest that even the more/most abstract live-action animated films paved the road, yellow-bricked or otherwise, toward the hybrid aesthetic that now dominates Hollywood. That road never veers too far from the West Coast, but then again, neither do the films themselves, many of which, not the least *Roger Rabbit*, constitute their own studies in and of Tinseltown (for a better view of live-action animated films across the Atlantic and beyond, see Frederick Litten's "Mixed Picture"). If these films narrativize and thematize the dynamic relationship between live action and animation in Hollywood from the mid-1900s to the early 2000s, then this study asks what kinds of stories those films tell. In Grinde's own midcentury appraisal, he imagines live action and animation as both combative (in the "infiltration of the cartoon technique" [26]) and simpatico ("democratic," "bi-partisan" [19]). Hopscotching alongside *Roger Rabbit*, I look at three successive phases in which live action and animation became better acquainted in Hollywood.

Chapter 1 focuses on hybrid films from the 1940s, 1950s, 1960s, and 1970s that *synchronized* live action and animation, as dance partners or duelists, in step or out of line. While cartoons paralleled live actors in the precise, choreographed asides of midcentury Technicolor musicals like *My Dream Is Yours* and *Mary Poppins*, animation was something to be feared and conquered in Harryhausen's dangerous fantasies. In 1946, Grinde qualifies "the flirtation between the little water color puppets and the members of the Screen Actors' Guild" as "mere puppy-love." "But just wait," he cautions, "until a few marriages have legalized things and you begin to meet these new couples socially. When they move into your own neighborhood theatre you'll know what's been going on right under your nose" (19).

Chapter 2 circles the cul-de-sac of 1990s and early 2000s films that *integrated* live action and animation, imagining them as sweethearts (*Casper*), teammates (*Space Jam*), and even family (*Alvin and the Chipmunks* and its squeakquels). The 1990s' and early 2000s' increasingly hybrid films domesticated animation, sometimes literally (and legally) through adoption. This amity was made possible, in large part, by advances in computer animation that Grinde could never have foreseen, allowing for a sustained and increasingly seamless meeting between live action and cartoons—Stanton's ever-blurring line—tilting into hybridity. In *Rocky and Bullwinkle*'s live-action/CG remake (2000), a narrator describes, up front, how the squirrel and moose depart 2D for "a strange new land where the line between cartoon and reality is so thin that it's hard to tell one from the other, . . . a place where, with the right special effects, it might just be possible to break through to the other side." By the 2000s, live action wasn't just difficult to distinguish from animation on-screen but off-screen as well, thanks to a more general drift to franchise-ready, platform-agnostic "content" (in 2010s parlance).

Chapter 3 circles back to the middle of the twentieth century and travels as far forward as the middle of the twenty-first to survey media that not only integrated live action and animation but *synergized* them in sprawling intellectual property mash-ups and match-ups. The intertextual crush of *Disneyland* (1954–58) and *The Wonderful World of Disney* (1991–) predicted films like *Ready Player One* and 2021's *Space Jam* sequel *A New Legacy*, which indiscriminately mix animated *and* live-action icons (Batman, Harryhausen's Cyclops and sword-wielding skeleton, Freddy Kreuger, Scooby Doo). These icons—more properly, properties—moved across live action and animation indiscriminately, erasing the thin line to which *Rocky and Bullwinkle* alludes. In both *Ready Player One*'s and *Space Jam*'s futures, as in *WALL·E*'s, the difference between live action and animation narrows to nil.

The conclusion lands, finally, in this future, where it's not only unnecessary but also sometimes impossible to announce any given film as part cartoon and part flesh, to recall Grinde's vision. Grinde himself settles on the fact that, "if art is supposed to be the concealment of effort, we should make an effort to conceal the effort" (26). Consider Disney's 2024 photorealistic prequel *Mufasa*: an all-cartoon production that looks all flesh—er, fur. The following pages trace how the live-action animated film moved toward concealment, in Gene Kelly's leaps and Roger Rabbit's bounds, over the course of a lively— and animated—century and then some.

1

SYNCHRONIZATION
(1919–1989)

In *Who Framed Roger Rabbit* (1988), Maroon Studios head R.K. (Alan Tilvern) enlists the private eye Eddie Valiant (Bob Hoskins) to investigate Jessica Rabbit (voiced by Kathleen Turner), wife to the studio's most super of stars, Roger (voiced by Charles Fleischer). Eddie, whose brother was killed by a Toon some years prior, resists all things animated. Naturally, he finds himself yoked to Roger—at one point handcuffed—as they're drawn into an ever-deeper mystery involving the duplicitous Judge Doom (Christopher Lloyd), who plans to raze Toontown, build a freeway, and reap the profits. During the film's climax, Doom's weaselly henchman string up Roger and Jessica, threatening to douse them with a lethal, green acid known as "Dip" (paint thinner by another name). Eddie must, in the end, get animated to save his partner from certain death, distracting Doom's stooges with a cartoonish song-and-dance routine set to "The Merry-Go-Round Broke Down," better known as the Looney Tunes theme. The henchmen die laughing before Eddie sets his sights on Doom, revealed to be a Toon in human disguise—the very Toon who murdered Eddie's brother, no less. Eddie's valiance stands in contrast to Doom's duplicity: Doom, hiding his cartoonishness within a live-action costume, dies; Eddie, wearing his newfound animatedness on his sleeve, lives. The film ends with Eddie, surrounded by the denizens of Toontown, gazing happily at its horizon. He smooches Roger for good measure.

Eddie and Roger's happy ending was a long time coming—and just plain long. *Roger Rabbit*'s press kit boasts of "over one thousand visual effects and fifty-seven minutes of interactive animation sequences, . . . the most technologically advanced example of combined live action and animation in film history" (Touchstone Pictures 19). Indeed, *Roger Rabbit* capped close to a century of cinema in which filmmakers yoked live action to animation, mostly in standalone shorts or in one-off scenes within longer features. For decades, live action and 2D animation mingled for no more than seven to ten minutes at a time, as in Disney's Alice comedies or Fleischer's Out of the Inkwell shorts, or else in the half-animated musical numbers—shorts hiding in plain sight—of

Anchors Aweigh (1945), *My Dream Is Yours* (1949), and *Dangerous When Wet* (1953). By 1964's *Mary Poppins* and 1971's *Bedknobs and Broomsticks*, that duration just barely doubled to twenty minutes, in both those films' musical live-action animated diversions. *Pete's Dragon* (1977) took a different tack, spreading its twenty-some minutes of blending across several discrete scenes, as had Ray Harryhausen's classical fantasies, like 1958's *The 7th Voyage of Sinbad* and 1963's *Jason and the Argonauts* before it—as had stop-motion spectacles like *The Lost World* (1925), *King Kong* (1933), and *Mighty Joe Young* (1949) before those. Throughout most of the twentieth century, live-action animated pairings stayed brief by necessity, since mixing flesh and ink variously involved bipacking (running two film strips through one camera at the same time), traveling mattes (combining two or more differently exposed images), and/or rear projection (shooting live actors in front of projected animated backgrounds). A single minute of *King Kong*, whose production involved both rear projection and early optical printing (to create film composites), could take upward of 150 hours to complete (Berman).

Yet, minute by minute, across nearly a hundred years, these fleeting meetings nudged Eddie and Roger closer to their eventual happy ending, a feature whose running time was *majority* mixed (56 of 104 minutes). Even while

Roger went long, its song-and-dance, human-versus-toon finale nodded to the dominant forms of the previously brief encounters that preceded it: duets and duels. When actors and cartoons met on-screen in the twentieth century, they either tangoed or they tussled; Joe Brady (Gene Kelly) leapt alongside Jerry Mouse in *Anchors Aweigh*, and Jason (Todd Armstrong) fended off skeletons in *Jason and the Argonauts*, maybe the midcentury's most iconic live-action animated match-ups. Given the extensive prep required for these meetings, live action and animation tended not to combine every day (sorry, Nick), not every scene, but in expensive, exceptional set pieces. These meetings were fleeting but pointed—on toe or by sword. All of *Roger Rabbit*'s precursors, whether dancers or fighters, foregrounded short but splendid *performances* where the physical coordination between live action and animation was paramount; live action kept pace with animation and vice versa, in complement and competition. In duets, live action and animation ran parallel to each other; in duels, they collided, perpendicular. These match-ups offered both what Grinde describes in "Greasepaint, Inkwell, and Co." as the "democratic intermingling" of live action and animation and the more aggro "infiltration" of the latter into the former (19, 26).

Grinde complains that most mixed films of his day lacked a "strong dramatic purpose" (19) in either their intermingling or infiltration. But live-action animated frolics and fracases were beside the point on purpose, novelty for novelty's sake. One 1924 exhibitor's catalog announced Disney's Alice comedies, "with Cartoons Co-ordinated into the Action," as "A Distinct Novelty"; a 1925 ad in *The Film Daily* heralded Alice as "HUMOROUS—NOVEL—NEW . . . WHAT A COMBINATION!!!" (Did anyone see Disney's Alice, let alone read Lewis Carroll, for the plot?) The combination of live action and animation remained surprisingly distinctive and novel for decades, in spite of (and sometimes because of) its dramatic purposelessness. A couple of decades after Alice, *The Three Caballeros'* "juxtaposition of humans and cartoon creatures" still struck *The New York Times*'s Bosley Crowther as "a cunning novelty" ("'Three Caballeros,' a Disney Picture"). Yet in a follow-up piece the next week, he described the film's blend of live action and animation as both "utterly specious and pointless" and "such as to make the wondering viewer gasp and thrill with incredulous surprise" ("'Three Caballeros' Shows"). A *New York Times* review of 1949's *My Dream Is Yours* likewise singles out the film's "cartoon fantasy sequence" as the "only bit of novelty in this hackneyed reworking of the how-tough-it-is-to-get-a-break-in-show-business theme" (T.M.P.). And, another twenty years later, Vincent Canby similarly singled out "the live-action-plus-cartoon sequence in Naboombu" as the "loveliest part" of the otherwise "aggressively friendly" *Bedknobs and Broomsticks.*

Throughout the mid-twentieth century, live-action animated scenes stood aside and stood out, taking tentative steps toward their eventual embrace in *Roger Rabbit.* J. P. Telotte notes that, in Robert Zemeckis's movie, Toons are "generally ostracized from the human world . . . relegated to the ghettolike Toontown" (*Animating Space* 188). This conceit, he says, reflects Hollywood history: "how animation, even within the precincts of a studio like Warner Bros., was often looked down on, treated as a separate—and lesser—entity" (Telotte, *Animating Space* 188). In Alan Cholodenko's investigation into *Who Framed Roger Rabbit,* he reiterates this "historical marginalization," with critics and scholars huddled on some "moral high ground with the 'photographed live action film,'" looking down on animation as a "form of graphic art unrelated to film or marginalizing it as an inferior, frivolous, merely mechanical form or appendage of film for children" (213). As Cholodenko and Roger's predecessors remind us, however, "It is only through animation that film can define itself as film. . . . Animation frames film" (Cholodenko 213). Viewed in this context, and viewed together, those predecessors create their own historical record of how Hollywood's live-action animated experiments slowly but surely drew live action and animation together, even in their separateness. Those experiments didn't so much resolve the tension between live action and animation (the business of Roger's successors, as we'll see in chapter 2) as they did hypothesize their similarity. And if they often turned to fantasy worlds or, like *Roger Rabbit*, some heightened version of Hollywood to stage their hypotheses, all the better to draw into question where live action ended and animation even began. Think of *King Kong*'s trajectory from a mysterious torch-lit island to Broadway's spotlights, from one fantastic precinct to another. Telotte sees, among *Roger Rabbit*'s many tricks, "a consistent foregrounding of the movies as a form themselves—an approach that interrogates their very artifice rather than trying to disguise it" (*Animating Space* 185). The experiments leading to *Roger Rabbit* used animated performances to underscore live-action artifice; they reminded audiences that they had, in fact, been watching a fantasy all along. Disney's Alice shorts and *Anchors Aweigh* and *Jason and the Argonauts* all suggested that moviemaking, in general, was indistinguishable from animation, a proposition made all the more believable as mixed pictures moved from Hollywood's margins to its mainstream. In the mid-century live-action animated film, then, we find a kind of synchronization every bit as crucial to film history as the coming of sound, the advent of color, or the pivot to digital, on whose cusp *Roger Rabbit* crouched.

SHORTS

Fleischer's and Disney's earliest live-action animated shorts showcase a performativity that would come to define the midcentury mixed picture. Hand-drawn characters shrug off the hand of the artist, stepping on or off frames or canvases that look very much like stages or screens-within-screens. They address their creators or else us; they fight with those creators, or else they dance for them (and for us). Indeed, these meandering, gag-driven films often look more like proofs of concept than proper shorts. Fleischer and Disney are still figuring out *why* to blend live action and animation—even if, in the meantime, they've figured out *how*. A little over a decade before Grinde's missive, the live-action animated technique is unequivocally novel, and it often revels, self-reflexively, in that novelty.

In *The Clown's Pup* (1919), the oldest surviving Out of the Inkwell short, Fleischer trades barbs with the joker who would become Ko-Ko. "That's pretty fair," the clown remarks, via world bubble, after we watch Fleischer hand draw and dress him. "What do you mean pretty fair?" Fleischer writes on the canvas. The clown pulls up his pantaloons and retorts, "You don't mean to say that this is high art." Here the clown and Fleischer engage in a quick draw: The former sketches a rough bulldog ("Looks like a full-blooded cruller," Fleischer writes) before the latter inks a more detailed mutt. The dogs—like proxies for their animated and live-action owners—fight each other; the clown watches from inside the frame, and Fleischer watches from without. When both dogs turn on the clown, he pleads for Fleischer to "open the bottle—quick!" All three drawings leap from the canvas into the inkwell, which Fleischer caps: a final, live-active period to this blended run-on sentence.

Alice's Wonderland (1923), Disney's earliest mixed short, proceeds in similar fashion—at least for its first half. The film begins not in the titular Wonderland but with Little Alice (Virginia Davis), "chuck [*sic*] full of curiosity," paying her "first visit to a cartoon studio" (so says the first intertitle). There she tells a young and dashing Disney, "I would like to watch you draw some funnies." Disney somewhat counterintuitively *stops* drawing as we (and he and Alice) watch his upright canvas animate: A doghouse coughs up its owner—exiled, we find out, by a fearsome feline inside. A delighted Alice applauds and gestures to another desk, whose canvas, laid flat, forms a stage for two upright, animated cat dancers and a three-piece feline band. We cut from this performance to a mixed-up scuffle: An animated mouse on a vertical canvas taunts a nearby, *live-action* tabby with an épée, then its tail; the cat eventually scrams from the pointed confrontation. In the third and final studio set piece, an animated cat and dog box each other, cartoonists crowding around the canvas to cheer them on (the dog triumphs). Another intertitle—"What Alice saw would make any little girl's heart flutter - - - so that night when the sandman came"—moves us from the studio to Alice's bedroom, where she falls asleep and into an all-animated dreamscape. Here, at last, is the wonder promised by the short's title: a Cartoonland populated by dogs, ducks, elephants, flamingos, and giraffes who watch as Alice disembarks from an animated train (in one shot, drawn; in another, a practical set made to look cartoonish). The animals' welcome banner—"LONG LIVE ALICE"—accidentally nods to their interloper's distinction, as the only "live" element of this otherwise animated world. The animals fete Alice in a parade; two rabbits hop in synchronized step for her. She repays the favor—"Now I will do a dance," reads the intertitle—on yet another stage, beneath a curtain strung between two trees, with mice on either side manning the ropes. Alice's dance arouses the attention of the Cartoonland Zoo's lions, who chase the young girl down a literal rabbit hole and then off a cliff. She wakes up before she hits rock bottom.

Pup and *Wonderland*, in their performance anxieties and ecstasies, set the template for later live-action animated efforts. If mixed pictures' charms depend on "the unexpected 'liveness' of the inanimate" (Connor), then Fleischer and Disney engineer scenarios that emphasize liveness: fights (clown vs. artist, cat vs. mouse, big cats vs. Alice) and dances (with Alice's prance in *Wonderland* paralleling the rabbits'). Both shorts' studio settings only underscore this seeming spontaneity: While we see Fleischer pen the clown, the clown soon takes up Fleischer's pen; when Alice asks to see Walt draw, his cartoons immediately carry on all by themselves. These performances obscure the labor that went into their making, with the clown's back-and-forth and Walt's cats and mice turning their artists into spectators just like us. In the live-action animated short, all the world's a stage.

Appropriately enough, then, subsequent mixed films take place in greater Hollywood—just as *Roger Rabbit* would many decades hence. *Hollywood Party* (1934), featuring one of the earliest blended segments in a feature-length picture (the norm for mixed experiments in the 1950s and 1960s), picks up, as its title suggests, at a star-studded soiree in that fabled land, where live action and animation mingle, if only for a moment. Its stars of the day include the Three Stooges, Laurel and Hardy, and, in a ninety-second cameo, Mickey Mouse, who stretches his nose in imitation of the party's host, Schnarzan (aka Jimmy Durante), giving a "ha-cha-cha-cha" for good measure. "An imposter!" Schnarzan panics. "Stealing my stuff!" Mickey responds with another Durante standby ("How mortifying!"), before socking his foil right in the (you guessed it) schnoz. Schnarzan/Durante grabs Mickey by the tail and flings him onto an opposite wall, where he razzes Schnarzan/Durante as the crowd begs him to (you guessed it again) perform. As an animated piano materializes, Schnarzan/Durante instructs Mickey to "cut out them adagios and play somethin' down to the level of these mugs!" We hear Mickey presumably tickling the ivories off-screen as a cartoon short, "The Hot Choclate Soldiers," plays out. In the short span of a minute and a half, Mickey levels with Durante, going from animated antagonist to accompanist.

The live-action animated Looney Tunes short *You Ought to Be in Pictures* (1940), a party more Hollywouldn't than Hollywood, ends less happily. The short begins with what appears, as first, to be the last handdrawn title card in the short's credits—"Warner Bros. Pictures Inc. Present Leon Schlesinger Productions. Home of LOONEY TUNES MERRIE MELODIES"; an abrupt cut reveals that this is, in fact, literal writing on the wall of Schlesinger's studio. We move inside that studio, where we briefly see an artist sketching Porky Pig, before a voice (an unmistakable Mel Blanc, aka Bugs Bunny) yells, "LUNCH!" The animators stream out of the building in fast motion, "much as cartoon characters might" (Telotte, *Animating Space* 166). Porky gets left behind with Daffy, who peels himself from his drawing board to bully the pig: "You call this a job? Working in cartoons? Pooh! I know where you can get a job in features as Bette Davis's leading man! Three grand a week!" Convinced, Porky jumps off his canvas, marches to the office of Leon Schlesinger—who apparently works through lunch— and asks to be released from his contract. "What's Errol Flynn that I haven't?" asks Porky. Schlesinger obliges but turns directly to the camera to assure the audience, "He'll be back." In order to reach the live-action sets, Porky must disguise himself as a live-action star (Hardy, har har); he makes his way to the filming of an elaborate ballroom dance scene (sans Bette Davis, sadly). In short order, Porky blows his cover and his nose, knocking a table of film-reel canisters over with a violent sneeze. Security tosses Porky from the live set, then the lot; there's no behind-the-scenes fraternizing here, as in *Roger Rabbit* (set less than a decade after this short). The poor pig hops into his cartoon jalopy and speeds away, nearly careening into an oncoming rush of horse-drawn carriages on the set of a western. Run off the dirt road, he wipes his forehead in relief: "I don't think I like this feature business.

Gee, I wonder if I can get my job back again." Back at the office, Daffy tries to impress Schlesinger with a manic song-and-dance; "Fred Astaire never could top this one," he belts, in a premonition of the live-action animated song-and-dance-offs (Kelly vs. Jerry, Day vs. Bugs, Williams vs. Tom and Jerry) yet to come. But back here, *You Ought to Be in Pictures*' takeaway is clear: animation's a headache that Schlesinger and company endure, rather than a partner that they embrace. Schlesinger waves Daffy off, and by short's end, the duck and pig are back to the drawing boards from which they emerged in the first instance. Yet Daffy and Porky's live-action hijinks, like Alice's and Ko-Ko's and Mickey's before them, intimate that, while different, "both drawn and live are similarly constructed, equally 'drawn' from nothing" (Telotte, *Animating Space* 165). Schlesinger's sign—heck, Schlesinger's animators—are both live action *and* animated.

ASIDES

Despite Porky's misgivings, cartoons began to pop up every so often—though never for very long—within live-action films in the 1940s. While Grinde cites *The Three Caballeros* as "about the only example" of live action and animation mixed in the same film at the moment of his writing, he leaves off another recent—and surely relevant—title from his survey. Released just a year before, Metro-Goldwyn-Mayer's romantic comedy *Anchors Aweigh* trails a pair of sailors (Frank Sinatra's Clarence Doolittle and Gene Kelly's Joe Brady) who spend four days of shore leave wooing the aspiring singer Susie Abbot (Kathryn Grayson). Critics praised a virtuosic two-and-a-half-minute scene midway through the film in which Joe dances alongside Jerry Mouse. "[Kelly] carries the film, and does an interesting routine in a phantasy sequence" (W.H.D.), said *The Wall Street Journal*; *The Washington Post*'s Sonia Stein commended Kelly's "vitality, control and buoyancy," which he shared with "a sad cartoon mouse in a delightful fairytale scene." Even Crowther was complimentary of Kelly and his "bright adagio with a little cartoon character in a trickily fanciful sequence (à la Disney) which fits well into this scheme" ("Anchors Aweigh"). The film made MGM a tidy profit and went on to receive five Oscar nominations, including for best picture and actor (Kelly), and won George Stoll the award for best score.

A handful of films followed in Kelly and Jerry's steps, which took $100,000 and several months to produce (Hess and Dabholkar 150); indeed, the prohibitive time and cost of the traveling matte process may have kept the pair's imitators to a minimum. Nevertheless, Warner Bros., which had let Porky and Daffy loose on Schlesinger in 1940, let Tweety and Bugs Bunny run amok with Doris Day and Jack Carson in a three-minute Easter-themed dream close to the climax of 1949's *My Dream Is Yours*. MGM, meanwhile, invited Jerry and Tom to swim with Esther Williams during an eight-minute dream scene in 1953's *Dangerous When Wet*, where, according to the star, the pink bubbles escaping from her lips alone cost $50,000; after telling Joseph Barbera that she could've blown the bubbles for free, the animator replied, "Yeah . . . but they wouldn't look real" (Williams 279)—as in, they wouldn't really look animated.

As we've already seen, critics often read these movies' mixed set pieces as parts separate from their live-action wholes. The *Times* review of *Dangerous When Wet*, for instance, nods to the "Tom and Jerry Cartoon in which a superimposed Miss Williams has an underwater adventure with the animal friends" as one of two "outstanding" sequences (Crowther, "Esther Williams"). To be fair, such scenes were often excepted by those films' writers and directors; a draft of the *My Dream Is Yours* screenplay, dated April 19, 1948 (Rivkin et al.), includes only a single line referencing scene 201, "BUGS BUNNY NUMBER," with no directions or dialogue beneath, probably because a separate director (the eminent animator Friz Freleng) handled it. Yet such exception disregards how these films use these scenes to *extend*, rather than altogether invent, a sense of cartoonish abandon. Mixed-media sequences in these movies do not so much interrupt your regularly scheduled program as they do remind you how of irregular that program was in the first place. *Anchors Aweigh* leads the charge here too, featuring many fixations of the midcentury mixed picture: dreams, analogies, kids, show business, and—relatedly—the fourth wall, against which it knocks just like Ko-Ko did all those years before. Never mind that these sequences appear in classic Hollywood musicals whose already-heightened realities involve intermittent songs that may or may not advance the plot but inveterately stress movement, rhythm, and synchronization. Animation, in this sense and in these scenes, affirms live action's capacity for fantasy, rather than vice versa. Tellingly, even later half-animated asides—in Kelly's own *Invitation to the Dance* (1956), in Disney's *Mary Poppins* and *Bedknobs and Broomsticks*—tilt all the way into fantasy.

We can trace those standout asides all the way back to Kelly and Jerry's tête-à-tête. *Anchors Aweigh* begins with a group of sailors' bodies made graphical as they march—forming first an anchor, then the word "NAVY." This demonstration preludes Clancy and Joe's anoint-ment, where they receive Silver Stars for their heroism before being granted shore leave; "I hate the thought of going ashore," Joe belts as he and Clarence head out the door to Hollywood, where the rest of the film takes place. And not just Hollywood—a number of scenes are set (so to speak) on the MGM backlot, where Clarence and Joe attempt to secure Susie an audition with the conductor José Iturbi, playing himself, as he often did in 1940s musicals (e.g., *Thousands Cheer*, *Two Girls and a Sailor*, and *Music for Millions*, all from 1944). Thus, the audience follows Clarence or Joe through throngs of technicians and extras, on and off soundstages, and then, in the very next scene, is asked to believe that the pair are dining on Los Angeles's famous Olvera Street and not on an MGM re-creation thereof (in that scene, we see the shadows of a band on a wall behind Clarence—looking very much like animated figures—as he sings "What Makes the Sunset"). At the same time that Clarence and Joe bop around the lot, Joe takes a shine to Susie's young nephew, a sailor-suited blond boy named Donald (played by Dean Stockwell), calling to mind Disney's duck; a "MUSICAL BREAKDOWN" in one of *Anchors Aweigh*'s earlier scripts actually lists a "DONALD DUCK-KELLY DANCE" in Gene and Jerry's stead (Kelly had initially asked Disney for help with the sequence; Lennart). It is Donald who serves as Joe's and our conduit to the half-animated world, when he asks Joe to tell his class how he earned his Silver Star. Joe, sitting beside a piano and in front of a blackboard scribbled over with cartoon figures, implores Donald and

his classmates, "Now close your eyes.... And try to imagine the most beautiful day you've ever seen. The greenest
grass and the singing-est birds and the shining-est sun....
Can you see it?" As Joe speaks, a fuzzy rectangular frame
forms on Donald's forehead, in which we see a row of
trees, and then Kelly (as Joe) skips by; the frame-within-
the-frame grows, filling the screen as Joe continues his
story. Are we in Donald's fantasy, or are we in Joe's? The
director, George Sidney, complicates this question ever
further, as Joe moves through the meadow in slight slow
motion—he "does some sensational turns and leaps,"
says the script (Lennart)—already abiding by a different kind of physics, then falls down a hole and crawls
through a tunnel to arrive in an even more cartoonish
meadow, a 2D castle in the background. Joe's mission,
which he accepts from a cadre of very Disney-like forest
creatures, is to petition the mouse king to allow dancing
and singing in this kingdom again. Joe disappears from
view in the foreground and reappears in the background
as an animated figure speeding up the stairs to Jerry's
tower. There, he and Jerry dance, in sync, to "The Worry
Song." But it's important to remember that Joe's act is
transgressive—he's breaking the law of the land. And
by breaking the law—teaching Jerry how to dance—he
abolishes that law, with the king bestowing an (appropriately) animated badge on him for his efforts. Joe's an

honorary toon. Sidney, for his part, is just as looney and just as transgressive, violating the rules of reality at every turn, compounding musical fantasy with childhood fantasy with Hollywood fantasy. At the film's end, he parallels the screen-within-a-screen that leads to the Kelly/ Jerry scene with shots of Susie singing (at last) for Iturbi, her face reflected in a camera lens and then bordered by the black outline of a camera's viewfinder. To swipe a line from Cholodenko's *Roger Rabbit* inquest, "These textual operations have vertiginous consequences" (223).

My Dream Is Yours and *Dangerous When Wet* are just as dizzying. The former concerns another aspiring singer (Doris Day as Martha Gibson) trying to make it in Los Angeles, while the latter follows an amateur swimmer (Esther Williams's Katy Higgins) trying to make it across the English Channel. If the title of Day's film nods to the relationship between Martha and her restless agent/love interest, Doug Blake (Jack Carson), it also serves as a pact between the film and the viewer, a recognition of a shared fantasy; not for nothing is Martha desperate to land herself on a radio show called *The Hour of Enchantment*. Like *Anchors Aweigh*, *My Dream Is Yours* plays fast and loose with fantasy and reality: Blake first hears Martha's voice through a mirrored jukebox adorned by an illustration of a sultry blonde; he assumes he's listening to a recording, but Martha is actually singing live from Metropolis

Music Co., where she works. Like Joe, Martha breaks the rules—she's supposed to *play* the songs, not *sing* them; so she gets sacked, and Blake rushes to take up her cause. In a reminiscence of *Anchors Aweigh*, he also takes up an interest in her and, by extension, in her son, Freddie, reading the boy a Bugs Bunny bedtime story at one point. This isn't the film's first mention of Warner Bros.' star: earlier, Blake says that "a couple of tone-deaf producers . . . couldn't tell Bing Crosby from Bugs Bunny," and later, Blake makes pasta while we hear Bugs's voice, on a record spinning in Freddie's bedroom, crooning, "What's cooking?" These winking mix-ups of live actors and cartoons presage Freddie's bedtime reverie, dreaming of Blake and his mother in funny bunny costumes, dancing alongside Bugs as the three sing, "Freddie, Get Ready" (the only song in the picture not sung on a stage or on the radio or at an audition—that is, naturalistically). As if to punctuate that fact, Freleng has Tweety Bird regard an inanimate, plush feline with his stock "I tawt I taw a puddy-tat"—but did he? As in *My Dream Is Yours* as a whole, the eyes and ears deceive.

Dangerous When Wet's cat and mouse run in the same circles. Katy arrives to an England so heavily shrouded by fog that we can only hear (not see) the press corps greeting her arrival; Katy and her family look much like the silhouettes on the wall in *Anchors Aweigh*. And the night before the planned Channel crossing, Katy and the other swimmers find themselves stuck in a rain so heavy that they might as well be underwater. Soon enough, Katy is: She falls asleep after reading her younger sister a comic about Tom and Jerry scuba diving, waking up in the sea. In this submerged and immersive medium, she swims alongside the pair, sees a seahorse family that looks like a caricature of her own, and fends off a suave octopus not unlike the sexy Frenchman (played by Fernando Lamas) who keeps interrupting her waking training. Underwater, Williams can move like a cartoon, with Tom and Jerry following her every whirl (contrast this with *Anchors Aweigh*, where a landlocked Joe greets Jerry's gravity-defying antics with consternation). This sequence implies that live action can also "make bodies dance, leap, float, and dive in a whimsical world with its own gravity"—hallmarks of animated performance, according to Donald Crafton (*Shadow of a Mouse* 5). And as in *My Dream Is Yours*, as in *Anchors Aweigh*, this cartoonish per-formativity runneth—or swimmeth—over, in a jarring shot where Katy, preparing to try on a bathing suit, draws the curtain on her audience, an anti-immersive gesture itself in line with animation's prankish "push-pull" (Crafton, *Shadow of a Mouse* 5).

Later animated asides doubled the length of their 1940s forebears while doubling down on those earlier films' sense of fantasy. The ambitious anthology *Invitation to the Dance* (1956), directed by Gene Kelly himself, features three dreamy, near-wordless dance sequences, the last of which stars Kelly as "Sinbad the Sailor" (Nathan Juran's Technicolor *7th Voyage*, with special effects by Harryhausen, would cast off a couple of years later). The segment begins, improbably, with Scheherazade (Carol Haney) sitting atop a blue box, in front of a blue screen—a nod to the special-effects method that enables Kelly to later travel, for some fifteen minutes, to an animated Arabia, care of Fred Quimby, William Hanna, and Joseph Barbera. Kelly arrives there on the heels of a young genie (David Kasday), whom he first encounters at a live-action port of call and with whom he shares a dancing duet, in matching sailor suits—an *Anchors* callback and Sinbad's first wish. His next wish whisks them to a storybook Arabia, where Sinbad duels and dances, sometimes at the same time, with a varied cast of cartoon characters. His first partner is a gravity-defying cartoon dragon who wraps Sinbad in its coils before the genie charms the raging reptile with a sweet song (just as he'd earlier charmed a puppeted cobra in the port of call). Sinbad does his best to match the dragon's sinewy movements, and he must do well enough, since the reptile seals their performance with a kiss on the cheek. Next, a pair of angry palace guards whisks Sinbad away, but the genie boy charms them, too. Sinbad ends up tapping in perfect step along-side the guards and their scimitars (substitutes for canes). From there, Kelly follows a beguiling harem girl outside, then into a flowered fantasy realm, performing a swirling, slow-motion dance with her (like the meadowed leaps in *Anchors Aweigh*). The guards interrupt this reverie, and Sinbad makes his way out of the palace alongside the pair, who flank him in an extended duet, their legs grow-ing long when he runs up some stairs, then shrinking in diminution when he comes back down. As soon as Sin-bad stops dancing, they give chase; only in sync, only in motion with them, is he safe. Sinbad gets a bright idea (a cartoon lightbulb appears above his head): He leads a sped-up routine so fast that the guards spin into abstract balls. He kicks the spheres off-screen and leaves, but not before the genie boy and the harem girl (now in her own sailor suit) join him in one last dance, the ratio reversed: two parts live action to one part animation—an inverse of his guarded two- (or three-) step. The little genie boy's pungi possesses the power to synchronize live action and animation—oh, ho, ho, it's magic.

Mary Poppins and *Bedknobs and Broomsticks'* slightly later and, at twenty-some minutes, slightly longer live-action animated segments appear in full-fledged fantasies, both drawn, not incidentally, from children's literature. In *Mary Poppins*, the practically perfect magical nanny and the Banks children enter an animated fantasia via one of Bert the chimney sweep's sidewalk drawings; in *Bedknobs and Broomsticks*, the witchy Miss Price and her charges journey to the Isle of Naboombu, where they land at the bottom of a lagoon before surfacing to watch a very animated football match. These scenes are diversions, not dreams; they intensify a fantasy or animation present in smaller moments, like the stop-motion toy-soldier march in *Poppins*'s sugary-sweet cleanup or Charlie's transformation from bunny to boy in *Bedknobs*. This intensification, in the end, may look less like *Anchors Aweigh* and more like a different kind of synchronization: a ride at Disneyland or Disney World (the latter of which opened the same year as *Bedknobs*), their own momentary, animated intensifications of the parks' live-action fantasy. Curiously, *Poppins* places its characters on carousel horses from which they take in their animated surroundings, while *Bedknobs*' sequence begins with its quartet passively looking at the lagoon from their bed, recalling Disney's *20,000 Leagues Under the Sea* or Pirates of the Caribbean attractions. Both *Poppins* and *Bedknobs* strive for a more prolonged, immersive mixed experience—an experience shared, coincidentally, not between one or two live actors and one or two cartoons but between dozens of cartoons and a quartet that looked very much like a nuclear family visiting Disneyland. As I've suggested elsewhere, theme parks cast riders as live-action actors alongside the attractions' own mechanical, digital, often animated performers (Meikle). In this respect, Disney's parks (which we'll revisit in chapter 3) analogize the half-and-half asides of the 1940s, 1950s, and 1960s, as highly choreographed, highly momentary, highly synchronized animated performances in otherwise live-action affairs. And just as Disneyland's magic circle (or hub) invites visitors to wonder where live-action ends and animation begins, so too do *Anchors Aweigh* and company's fantasy-land tours.

IN-BETWEENERS

Several live-action animated sequences that ran parallel to *Anchors Aweigh* and *My Dream Is Yours* in the 1940s raised the same question. Interestingly, these sequences appeared in their own progenitors to Disneyland and Disney World: Disney's package pictures, so called because they "packaged together various short cartoons, were typically episodic, often depended heavily on musical numbers, and used live-action scenes to link their animated sequences—or animation to link their live-action elements" (Telotte, *Animating Space* 143). While Grinde neglects to mention *Anchors Aweigh* in "Greasepaint, Ink-well & Co.," he briefly refers to Disney's "second entry in the new medium" after *The Three Caballeros*: "Uncle Remus," the working title for 1946's *Song of the South* (not a package picture per se but a live-action film still built around three interlinked cartoon shorts). Along with *The Three Caballeros*, *Song of the South* appeared in the midst of Disney films—*The Reluctant Dragon* (1941), *Saludos Amigos* (1942), *Make Mine Music* (1946), *Fun and Fancy Free* (1947), *Melody Time* (1948), and *The Adventures of Ichabod and Mr. Toad* (1949)—that strung together disparate cartoon shorts, sometimes threading the needle with live-action animated scenes.

These so-called package pictures represented a necessary evil for a Disney debilitated by wartime staff shortages, budget cuts, and a contentious strike: "by incorporating live-action elements," writes Telotte, "animators had to draw fewer images, thereby reducing costs and, in some instances, speeding up production" (*Animating Space* 142). If live-action animated scenes were expensive, they were, at least, cheaper than feature-length animated films, hence why 1942's *Bambi* was Disney's last such production until 1950's *Cinderella*. Such scenes also allowed Disney to differentiate its product from yet one more encroaching threat—that of television, which was not well suited to blending live action and animation, "for technological as well as economic reasons" (Smoodin 105). (Richard Donner and Friz Freleng's failed pilot for *Philbert* [1963], featuring a live-action cartoonist bedeviled by one of his cartoon creations, stands as a rare midcentury attempt at live-action animated TV outside of commercials.) The package pic offered Disney some cheap, but relatively expensive, distinction.

Disney's thrift came at a cost. Eric Smoodin singles out *The Three Caballeros* as "the first of the Disney features to receive generally unfavorable reviews" (105), a claim that Grinde's complaints in *The Screen Writer*'s pages bear out, as does John Mason Brown's carp, in *The Saturday Review*, about *Caballeros*' "unhappy mixture" of humans and cartoons (qtd. in Smoodin 105). In the 1940s, Smoodin says, "Disney began losing favor with the critics, at least in part because they no longer believed in his powers of reconciliation"—between "art and commerce, high art and low art" (100–101)—and, as these reviews make clear, between live action and animation. Crowther's spanking assessment of *Song of the South* (which includes no fewer than five "whams" meant to mimic hand-on-backside) reminds Disney that his "art and forte is entirely in the animated cartoon. . . . Although we have anxiously tolerated your previous 'live action' escapades, we have never particularly admired them—and we certainly never thought they'd lead to this" ("Spanking Disney"). A *Time* writer concludes, after enduring *Fun and Fancy Free*, that "in spite of the Disney technical skill, it has never been a very good idea to mix cartoons and live actors" (qtd. in Smoodin 105). If critics discussed Disney "in terms of oppositions" in the 1940s, says Smoodin, "they were usually irreconcilable" (102).

Whatever the critical opprobrium of Disney's 1940s films, they shared some of the live-action animated asides' early tendencies while stretching toward the live-action animated film's feature-length future. *Song of the South* is as emblematic of this cycle as *Anchors Aweigh* is of its. Disney's film does not take place in Hollywood but in its own "historical never-never land" (Telotte, *Animating Space* 148), a post–Civil War Georgia seemingly free from racial strife. As in Hollywood, stories are also paramount there, and none more so than those of Uncle Remus (James Baskett), whose Brer Rabbit tales inspire the three aforementioned cartoon shorts. Remus relates these stories to young Johnny (Bobby Driscoll) and sometimes his friends Ginny (Luana Patten) and Toby (Glenn Leedy). In one scene that recalls *Anchors Aweigh*'s push into Donald's forehead, the directors, Harve Foster and Wilfred Jackson, iris in on Johnny's face as Remus begins telling his tale; the image crossfades between Johnny and Brer Fox's animated lair, irising out on the latter.

Just as *Anchors Aweigh*'s mind games raise the question of whose fantasy we're in, so does *Song of the South*'s (Johnny's or Remus's?). But the later film's questioning

goes further, crossfading between live action and animation throughout. Remus first happens upon Brer Rabbit
in an animated landscape, after singing "Zip-a-Dee-Doo-
Dah"; as if trying to convince not just Johnny but us, he
croons, "It's the truth / It's actual," while a top-hatted
toon bluebird perches on his shoulder. Remus and Rabbit are initially separated by a run-down fence, but the
latter hops atop and then over it, shaking hands with the
former on his way: a human/toon accord. As Brer Rabbit disappears into the animated background, the film
transitions to its first cartoon short, which concludes
with a crossfade between Brer Rabbit's home at night
and Remus's face, moonlike in the sky above. Before the
second short, Remus jaunts through the country singing "How Do You Do?" alongside another fence that's
sometimes live action and sometimes animated. This
"*reciprocity* of space," Telotte suggests, makes it "almost
impossible to tell where the real rail ends and the animated one begins" (*Animating Space* 149)—one early
instance of later live-action animated hybridity. The film's
closing revels in this irreconciliation when Brer Rabbit
and friends hop into the real world itself, encountering
Johnny, Ginny, and Toby along their own country road.
Remus can hardly believe his eyes. "Mr. Bluebird's on my
shoulder," sings Johnny this time around; Remus drops
the logs he's holding and turns directly to the camera

as he repeats, "It's the truth / It's actual." Who are we to argue?

Fun and Fancy Free likewise pries at the fence separating live action from animation, this time from a perch in the Hollywood Hills. Before we even reach the house way up there where we meet Jiminy Cricket, he's listed, in the film's credits, alongside cartoons (Donald Duck, Mickey Mouse), humans (Patten, *Song of the South*'s Ginny), and something in between (Charlie McCarthy and Mortimer Snerd, Edgar Bergen's famed ventriloquist dummies). The hand-drawn "Featuring" title card polices the separation between the livelier stars (McCarthy, Snerd, Patten) and their more animated counterparts (Duck, Mouse, Cricket) only by a thin blue line. That line further thins as we pick up with Jiminy in the Hollywood house, drawn in nearly photo-realistic detail.

Jiminy comes across a "deadpan doll and a droopy bear," sad, inanimate toys that he tries to enliven by spinning "A Musical Story sung by Dinah Shore": "Bongo," the film's first cartoon short. As the record starts, Jiminy somehow converses with the prerecorded Shore, animation and live action already in (improbable) lockstep. After the record ends, Jiminy discovers an invitation for a party at "the house across the way," which he espies through a window frame within the frame. Like Brer Rabbit hopping the fence, Jiminy drops outside and heads to the neighboring home, whose exterior is photo-realistically animated but whose interior—which *we* espy through another window frame—is live-action. Jiminy sneaks inside, where he and we watch Bergen, with a squinched forefinger and thumb, animate a literal hand puppet named Ophelia, much to the delight of Patten as well as Snerd and McCarthy (both sitting some distance from Bergen). "Isn't that a wonderful trick?" Patten asks McCarthy, both highlighting and sidestepping the dummy's own implicit trickery.

While Jiminy reclines in a piece of live-action silverware, Bergen, now astride Snerd, introduces the second cartoon short ("Mickey and the Beanstalk"), imploring Mortimer to "paint a mental picture" of the story's Happy Valley. An undulating cartoon blob appears over Snerd's head, with a dog melting into a mountaintop melting into train melting into a lighthouse and boat and desert island. He gives up and Patten gives it a go, in a moment that again brings to mind *Anchors Aweigh*'s Donald and (now) *Song of the South*'s Johnny. "Yes, I think I can see it, Mr. Bergen," she says as a pastel cloud slowly overtakes the screen, leading into the cartoon. "It's beautiful." Before the introduction of the story's foe—Willie the Giant in this *Jack and the Beanstalk* riff—Patten asks Bergen what the leviathan looked like, and the film cuts to Bergen's excellent shadow-puppet approximation. The image of Bergen's projection crossfades into the giant's animated shadow, and we follow his exploits right up until Mickey sends him tumbling down the beanstalk. Slain in the short, the behemoth reappears in *Fun and Fancy Free*'s conclusion, prying the roof off of Bergen's house to inquire if the party's seen "a teency-weency little mouse." The last we see of Willie, meanwhile, he's traipsing past Grauman's Chinese Theatre and wearing the Brown Derby's Brown Derby out, the Hollywood sign blinking in the background. Willie's exit adverts to "the obvious constructions of Hollywood," serving as "a stylistic reminder of how elusive the real is, and how *illusive* all that movie culture constructs for us also is" (Telotte 153–154). Like *Song of the South*'s final "It's actual," Cliff Edwards and the Starlighters punctuate Willie's goodbye by urging the audience to "Believe in all [their] dreams," even—and maybe especially—those most animated of reveries.

Unlike *Anchors Aweigh* and company, *Fun and Fancy Free* and *Song of the South* don't restrict such reveries to brief asides, instead extending them across a series of scenes that look, in sum, like full live-action animated films. Disney's package (and package-adjacent) films drove mixed pictures closer to feature length by using live-action animated scenes as main roads rather than detours.

FEATURES

Elsewhere in "Greasepaint, Inkwell, & Co.," Grinde mentions a King Arthur project in development that will feature not only the "top players of the day" but also a dragon that "will be no papier-mâché lizard" but rather "the ferocious reptile right out of the book" (21). Of the project's "half bird half beast" harpy, Grinde writes, "Central Casting won't have to bother over this confused fauna, and neither will the zoo. It will be undiluted essence of inkwell" (21).

The passion project, from the famed animator Hugh Harman, never ascended from development hell, but Grinde's mention of it here glances at those half-animated films that made the greatest strides toward feature length in the middle of the twentieth century: movies based on myths and legends. With rare exception (e.g., the Id monster in 1956's *Forbidden Planet*, brought to life by animators on loan from Disney's effects department [Clarke and Rubin 34]), those movies were drawn not from the inkwell but rather from clay and plasticine, in stop-motion fantasies that combined live action and animation in 3D. If Grinde doesn't allude to such films in his missive, it may only be because, in 1945, they were far scarcer than live action and 2D combinations; a full fifteen years separated *King Kong* and *Son of Kong*, both 1933, from their acolyte,

Mighty Joe Young (1949). Only during the 1950s' B-movie sci-fi boom would plasticine (or something like it) take center stage in films like *The Beast from 20,000 Fathoms* (1953), *It Came from Beneath the Sea* (1955), and *20 Million Miles to Earth* (1957), all featuring creatures from the special-effects impresario Harryhausen, who'd worked on *Mighty Joe*. Like *King Kong*, such movies tended to view animation as an isolated threat to be dealt with rather than a constant presence. But by the 1960s and 1970s, that threat became more widespread and more insistent, with stop-motion monsters populating entire fantasylands in *Jason and the Argonauts* and Sinbad's subsequent voyages, like 1973's *Golden Voyage* and 1977's *Eye of the Tiger*.

The first *Sinbad* pic, Juran's *7th Voyage*, boasts no fewer than six distinct stop-motion creations, including Harryhausen's famed Cyclops; a blue snake-woman who performs a hypnotic dance; a two-headed, newborn roc (the giant bird of Arabian lore); a bigger, badder roc; a sword-fighting skeleton, a precursor to *Jason*'s equally famous crew; and a chained dragon. As this list suggests, animation remained a menace in *7th Voyage*, much as it had been—from twenty thousand fathoms, from beneath the sea, or from twenty million miles away—before. But that threat was aberrant in Harryhausen's earlier work: an animated incursion into an otherwise peaceful live-action world, not unlike the blended asides of 1940s and

1950s musicals. Here, the creatures—and animation itself—were endemic to *7th Voyage*'s Colossa and Baghdad. *7th Voyage* and its mythic ilk offered not *intrusive* but *immersive* fantasies, to borrow Farah Mendlesohn's distinction between those stories in which "the fantastic enters the fictional world" and those in which "we are allowed no escape" from the fantasy (xiv). In *7th Voyage*, Sinbad (and his audience) cannot abscond from fantasy/animation; we're always dreaming. More akin to the long cons of Disney's package pictures than *Anchors Aweigh* or *Mary Poppins*, Juran's film invites animation to sprawl across multiple scenes, lending a blended air to the entire affair. Throughout *7th Voyage*'s hour and a half, Harryhausen's various stop-motion monsters appear in eight different sequences, each ranging in length from one to ten minutes (even if the duration of the actual animated shots amounts to far less). At any given moment in *7th Voyage*, animation could be hiding just around the corner. And animation is often hiding in plain sight, as in the subplot involving the evil Sokurah (Torin Thatcher) shrinking Princess Parisa (Kathryn Grant) to the size of mouse; her fun-size exploits owe to Dynamation, the same rear-projection process that allows Sinbad's company to tussle with the Cyclops.

7th Voyage may, on the whole, present a fraught picture of live-action animated relations, but friendship seems at least possible in a couple of its successors. Juran's 1962 film *Jack the Giant Killer* borrows *7th Voyage*'s Sinbad (Kerwin Mathews) and Sokurah (Thatcher) as its titular lead and its evil foe, the sorcerer Pendragon. The film begins with Pendragon gifting another princess, Elaine (Judi Meredith), a music box in the shape of a castle turret, from which emerges a diminutive jester, animated by stop-motion. "Why, he could almost be alive!" Elaine exclaims before mimicking the jester in a courtly dance—a duet. Alas, the accord is short-lived. While Elaine is sleeping, Pendragon bewitches the jester, now at her bedside, with a burst of electric red and blue 2D-animated flames. The jester makes off with Elaine after transforming into a giant barely discernible from Harryhausen's Cyclops. Indeed, *Jack the Giant Killer* looked *so* much like *7th Voyage* that Columbia (the latter film's distributor) threatened to sue *Jack*'s producer, Edward Small. To avoid litigation and distinguish the film from its forebear, Small recut *Jack* as a musical (of sorts), dubbing over dialogue with "sung" lines and inserting songs over the movie's action scenes. This literal remix has the perhaps unintended effect of turning the movie's duels *into* duets, as when Jack confronts Pendragon—making good on his name by transforming into a hulking stop-motion reptile—at *Jack*'s end. In a discordantly jaunty song attributed to Jack's leprechaun helper (played by Don Beddoe), the imp encourages our hero: "Stick out your chin, force a grin, you're gonna win! / Soon you will discover / he's running for cover."

Harryhausen himself came close to going musical in 1969's *The Valley of Gwangi*, which teases a circus act by a miniature horse (actually a prehistoric Eohippus) named El Diablo, the rare Harryhausen creation, as Astrid Goldsmith points out, probably modeled to scale (Fantasy/ Animation, "Episode 33"), not unlike *Jack's* jester. To a music-box tinkle much like that film's as well, El Diablo's keeper explains her plan to have the horse waltz, in a miniature dome, atop a full-size white steed. Alas, El Diablo is stolen back to the film's eponymous valley (where lurk Harryhausen's more typical, terrible lizards) before we get to witness this live-action animated duet.

These stop-motion movements mirrored a friendliness more obvious in the scant live-action 2D features of the 1960s and 1970s, including *The Incredible Mr. Limpet* (1964), Gene Kelly's own *Jack and the Beanstalk* (1967), and *Pete's Dragon* (1977). In *Limpet*, Don Knotts's title character loves fish so much that he turns into one after a fateful tumble off of a Coney Island dock. The fishy but still bespectacled 2D Limpet possesses the power to roar—or "thrum"—loudly, and he becomes an asset to the US Navy, which had earlier stamped the fleshy Limpet with a 4F. *Limpet* tends to separate the impossible, animated physics of Limpet's underwater escapades from live action, but midway through the film, he surfaces to hear tell of the United States' entry into World War II. He resurfaces to offer his services to a US warship targeting a U-boat; after the hit lands, a skeptical naval officer admits that the voice—whom- or whatever it belongs to—is "friendly and cooperative. . . . It wants to work with us." Live action and animation cooperate not just in Limpet's service but in essence: The US warship is live action from afar, but its underside is animated (in something approximating realism) as Limpet swims by—constructed, from top to bottom, with mixed materials. A later montage, in which Limpet imagines himself as both a live-action and animated decorated general, concludes with a graphic match between a real military plane and an identically shaped cartoon manta ray that knocks Limpet out of his daydream. Live action and animation aren't just comrades in arms but part of the same winged ecology.

In Kelly's musical *Jack and the Beanstalk*, produced by Hanna/Barbera, Jack (Bobby Riha) still battles a giant, but the magic-bean peddler Jeremy (Gene Kelly) also frees the 2D Princess Serena from her harped prison with a live-action animated kiss. In one early scene, Jeremy encourages Jack to swap his beans by singing a plucky tune called "Vice Versa," which serves as a kind of thesis statement for the film. That night, a 2D animated vine pokes through Jack's window to tickle his nose. When he runs outside to see the beanstalk, its base is live action, but when the camera angles up to reveal its extent, the frame's entirely animated. When Jack asks where it goes, the peddler replies, "Yonder, perhaps . . . betwixt, between." It leads, of course, to a series of blended set pieces betwixt and between live action and animation: Jack and the peddler dancing, in sync, across the painted landscape in the clouds (to a reprise of "Vice Versa"); Jeremy tangoing, in sync with two cartoon "Woggle-Bird" minions, flanking him like the guards in "Sinbad the Sailor"; Jack leading an army of animated mice in a synchronized military march; Jeremy dancing with Serena in a dreamy ballet. When Jeremy, Serena, and Jack hit a dead end in their escape from the giant's castle—a too-high door handle—one of the animated mice pipes up: "Hey," he says to Jack, "remember what you said about doing something all together that no one could do by himself?" The toon mice form a pyramid that Jeremy ascends to break free—more live-action animated cooperation.

Pete's Dragon represents maybe the most direct link between these live-action 2D features and their stop-motion contemporaries; the film was directed by Don Chaffey, who'd helmed *Jason and the Argonauts* and 1966's caveman fantasy *One Million Years B.C. Pete's Dragon* revolves around the friendship between a young orphan (played by Sean Marshall) and his not-so-imaginary dragon, Elliott (snuffs and grunts provided by Charlie Callas), a friendlier reptile than any of Harryhausen's. Elliott conveniently possesses the power to turn invisible, meaning he's unanimated for much of the film—with the mixed segments' length equal, in the end, to *Bedknobs*' or *Poppins*'s. But he's visible for an early duet with Elliott—"Boo Bop Bop Bop Bop (I Love You, Too)"— and remains a constant, if not always on-screen, presence throughout the movie. Elliott reveals himself to many of the movie's townsfolk at *Pete's Dragon*'s climax, relighting an extinguished lighthouse lamp with his fiery breath. "Elliott, I could give you a great big kiss," says Nora, the lighthouse keeper's daughter, and she does, just as Eddie locks lips with Roger at *Rabbit*'s end.

OPPOSITES

The exact same week that *Roger Rabbit* premiered in June 1988, the pop star Paula Abdul released *Forever Your Girl*, her debut album. The next year, Roger and Paula would become forever linked when Abdul's music video for "Opposites Attract," the LP's sixth single, hit MTV. In the video, Abdul trades moves—and verses—with the suspendered MC Skat Kat, a cartoon riff not only on Roger but on *Anchors Aweigh*'s Jerry before him. Abdul's cool lament at the single's beginning, "Baby, it seems we never ever agree," doubles its meaning on-screen: Abdul isn't just trying to reconcile with her lover; she's trying to reconcile live action and animation. Just as Roger and Eddie move from foes to friends in fits and starts, Abdul and Skat Kat oscillate between gibing and jiving; throughout the video's three and a half minutes, the pop star engages in a visual, and sometimes physical, tug-of-war with her 2D admirer. When we first see the pair together on the video's noirish, neon set, Skat Kat taps his finger on Abdul's shoulder, where it burns and bursts into a flurry of animated flames; Abdul leaves him cold, slamming a door after she struts away. They reunite more happily atop an alley wall, in silhouette (like *Anchors Aweigh*'s shadows), performing a fleet routine in which Abdul tugs Skat Kat's tail and spins him into a cartoon blur. In the next segment, however, the camera shifts between the pair—they no longer share a frame—as they stare straight at the camera, trading lines: "Who'd have thought we could be lovers? / She makes the bed, and he steals the covers." One of the next scenes picks up on this suggestiveness, with Skat Kat reclined in Abdul's lap on a loveseat. "I don't like cigarettes," she complains, removing a butt from his lips. "I like to smoke," he replies, exhaling live-action fumes into her face, paying her back for the burn, the smoke after the fire—inviting a kind of chemical equivalence between the pair. Skat Kat flips on top of Abdul, pinning her wrists to the white leather as they both look at the camera: "Things in common? There just ain't one / But when we get together, we have nothin' but fun." Abdul sits up, wringing Skat Kat's neck. He reaches toward the camera and draws a curtain—not unlike Katy in *Dangerous When Wet*—transporting the singer and MC to an animated staircase, where they two-step together. Like *Roger Rabbit*, "Opposites Attract" speculates that maybe, just maybe, live action and animation could be foes *and* friends (and maybe more). In "Opposites Attract's" chemical equation, Abdul and her Kat remain at odds but even. After nearly a century of sporadic duets and duels, of carefully calibrated choreography, live action and animation "come together," as the chorus goes: "you know it ain't fiction, just a natural fact."

2

INTEGRATION (1989–2021)

Who Framed Roger Rabbit wrapped 1988 as the highest grossing movie in the United States; only *Rain Man* earned more worldwide. In one year-end top-ten list, Roger Ebert praised Robert Zemeckis's film as "a virtuoso combination of live action and animation" ("Best 10 Movies"), lauding it alongside *A Fish Called Wanda* and *The Accidental Tourist*, movies whose company *Roger Rabbit* would keep at the following year's Oscars. There, it picked up three prizes, for film editing, sound effects editing, and visual effects, as well as a Special Achievement Award for Richard Williams's animation.

Despite *Roger Rabbit's* commercial, critical, and awards successes, however, the film never inspired anything like an obvious follow-up. A proposed prequel pitting Roger against real-life Nazis, provisionally titled *The Toon Platoon*, languished in development hell. In the meantime, Roger cameoed in a couple of retrospective specials, *Mickey's 60th Birthday* (1988) and *The Best of Disney: 50*

Years of Magic (1991), both reminiscent of *Fun and Fancy Free* (1947) in their intermittent, interstitial mix of live action and animation. The rabbit's silver-screen exploits, meanwhile, were restricted to a trio of animated shorts— 1989's *Tummy Trouble*, 1990's *Roller Coaster Rabbit*, and 1993's *Trail Mix-Up*—that played before the contemporaneous live-action features *Honey, I Shrunk the Kids* (1989), *Dick Tracy* (1990), and *A Far Off Place* (1993). These diversions mimicked *Who Framed Roger Rabbit*'s opening (a cartoon short starring Roger and Baby Herman called *Somethin's Cookin'*) without ever repeating its dizzying fourth-wall break (before the short's over, a frustrated Baby Herman storms off-screen, into the real world). This arrangement kept Roger, and animation in general, at arm's length from live-action. Roger was no longer the star attraction, and neither was the combination of live action and animation that made his introduction so distinctive in the first place. Just as Disney's mixed package pictures like *Fun and Fancy Free* had underwritten the studio's feature animation comeback with *Cinderella* some forty years before, the renaissance that followed *Roger Rabbit*'s release, starting with 1989's *The Little Mermaid* and continuing with *Beauty and the Beast* (1991) and *Aladdin* (1992), was strictly animated. Amid this renaissance, 2D/live-action fare went underground, as in the sex-obsessed *Volere Volare* (1991), *Cool World* (1992), and

Evil Toons (1992)—all more indebted to Jessica Rabbit than Roger.

Roger's cotton-tailed retreat was hastened, at the same time, by a somewhat less traditional form of animation. As J. P. Telotte avers, "[*Roger Rabbit*] appears at precisely the time when the new digital technologies were starting to have an influence—on both live-action and animated film" (*Animating Space* 183). Artists achieved the ethereal sweep of *Beauty and the Beast*'s ballroom sequence, for instance, using Disney's/Pixar's Computer Animation Production System (CAPS). But digital animation also began a protracted dance with live action, bringing sweeping changes to multiplex screens in the 1990s. The *Roger Rabbit* animator Tom Sito describes how, by the middle of that decade, the "Gettysburgs" of digital animation—*Terminator 2: Judgment Day* (1991), *Jurassic Park* (1993), and *Toy Story* (1995)—had made computer graphics (CG) "a household word" (266). Even Zemeckis himself quickly moved on from 2D, tinkering with CG in 1992's *Death Becomes Her* and 1994's *Forrest Gump*. The film scholar Stephen Prince notes that while computer graphics had appeared in earlier films like *Westworld* (1973) and *Tron* (1982), *Jurassic Park* represented a moment when digital animation "became salient in the imagination of popular audiences," not to mention "a new engine for box office growth" (9).

Such titles were clearly indebted to at least *one* strain of live-action animated film: The original *Terminator* (1984), for instance, used stop-motion to animate the T-800 cyborg before the T-1000's digital upgrade in *T2*. And for *Jurassic Park*, Steven Spielberg enlisted the animators Phil Tippett and Craig Hayes to explicitly "bridge the gap" between "traditional stop motion animation" and "computer graphics-based visual effects" (Tippett Studio), resulting in a series of screen tests featuring Harryhauseneque dinosaurs. Tim Burton, who'd so memorably employed stop-motion in 1988's *Beetlejuice*, himself pivoted to CG in 1992's *Batman Returns* and again in 1996's *Mars Attacks!* This pivot made sense: While CG shared stop-motion's interest in the third dimension, it could smooth the stuttered movements that made Harryhausen's and *Beetlejuice*'s creatures so uncanny. But where did this unflattened landscape leave the two-dimensional Roger, to say nothing of the live-action animated film that *he* epitomized?

A more panoramic view of that landscape—one encompassing not just digital animation's Gettysburgs but several of its lesser-known battlefields—reveals that, even as Roger burrowed underground, he left his fingerprints (if not footprints) all over CG's fronts. *Space Jam* (1996) both riffed on *Roger* and made "a quantum leap beyond [that] landmark" in mixing live action, 2D animation,

and 3D CG imagery (Jackson). The *Roger Rabbit* alum
Ed Jones boasted that *Space Jam* was "the largest project
ever to use so much mixed media" (qtd. in Jackson), pre-
dicting that the film would supersede its predecessor as
the new standard for live-action animated productions;
Jones's colleague Bruce Smith described *Space Jam's*
technological leap as "the gulf war of animation" (qtd.
in Jackson). An earlier, even more spirited *Roger Rabbit*
successor—1995's *Casper*—broached the 2D/3D gulf
by reanimating a flat comic book icon as a rounded-out
star, the first CG lead of his era. *Cinefantastique's* Dan Persons ventured that "even if you had somehow coaxed Jeff
Goldblum into bugging out his eyes and stuttering 'P-p-
p-p-p-pp-pleez,' you couldn't get a more unusual meeting
of WHO FRAMED ROGER RABBIT and JURASSIC PARK
than Universal's CASPER" (14).

Casper preceded some dozen blockbusting remakes
in the late 1990s and early 2000s, including *Scooby Doo*
(2002), *Garfield* (2004), and *Alvin and the Chipmunks*
(2007), wherein the cartoon stars of yesteryear traded
2D for computer-generated 3D, adapting to their newly
live-action environments. Like Roger, Scooby and crew
looked to animation's past to forge its future. Just a few
miles from the Gettysburgs of the digital revolution that
made CG a household word, Roger's successors brought
CG home by way of Saturday mornings. Sure, some

critics complained that those successors treated their 2D inspirations no better than doormats; in a representative objection, *The Wall Street Journal*'s Joe Morgenstern wrote that *Casper* "come[s] up short" as a feature film but is "truly haunting" as "an infomercial." But audiences walked right in: *Casper* was the eighth highest grossing movie worldwide in 1995, *Space Jam* the eighteenth highest in 1996, *Scooby Doo* the fifteenth highest in 2002, *Garfield* the twenty-fifth highest in 2004, and *Alvin* the fourteenth highest in 2007.

Even if Roger himself was scarce in the 1990s and early 2000s, then, Zemeckis's film cast a long, leporine shadow over those decades' ascendant blockbusters. Such blockbusters not only followed *Roger*'s lead in drawing out the combination of live action and animation beyond isolated scenes and set pieces (like Gene and Jerry's dance, Esther and Tom and Jerry's swim, or Mary's jolly holiday) to feature length. They also, like *Roger*, featured narratives that reconciled live action with animation. *Who Framed Roger Rabbit* isn't just a mystery but a buddy cop movie— shucks, a romantic comedy—in which live action and animation reluctantly discover their love for each other (sealed with that kiss between Eddie and Roger at the film's end). *Casper*, *Space Jam*, and *Alvin and the Chipmunks* similarly revolve around tales of teamwork, acceptance, and integration—not just between live action and animated characters but also between live action and animation in general. Whereas CG often amounts to a threat in *Jurassic Park* (much like the stop-motion in Harryhausen's fantasy films), Roger's followers use CG to bridge the gap between live action and animation, sometimes literally: In *Space Jam*'s climactic basketball match-up, Michael Jordan delivers a game-winning dunk with a cartoonishly outstretched, full-court-length arm (made possible by CG). Paul Wells remarks that, in order for Jordan to become an even greater superstar than he already is, number 23 has "to be animated . . . to be excess" (Fantasy/Animation, "Episode 70"). Jordan's fate—or fortune—looks much like Eddie's at *Roger*'s end, when the intrepid detective gets looney to thwart Doom's weasels. A survey of CG's lesser-known battlefields reveals how Roger led the charge in forging this accord—this truce—between live action and animation. Following over half a century in which animation had intruded, as a musical novelty or fantastical threat, in live-action films, Roger's CG pursuivants came to a (presumably joy-buzzered) handshake agreement with animation—a handshake whose buzz would reverberate for decades to come, in Hollywood's default hybrid blockbusters.

COOL WORLD

Roger Rabbit's most immediate successor, however, was more handsy than handshaking. When the animator Ralph Bakshi's louche *Cool World* debuted in July 1992, several critics unfavorably compared the pic to its Disney/Touchstone predecessor. *The Christian Science Monitor*'s David Sterritt described *Cool World*'s blend of animation and live action as "hopelessly vulgar in ways never dreamed of by 'Who Framed Roger Rabbit.'" *The Baltimore Sun*'s Stephen Hunter complained, "Unlike 'Who Framed Roger Rabbit,' [*Cool World*] never seriously establishes the ground rules of the principle of transference or the relationship between [the real and animated world], and so what follows is gibberish." And *The New York Times*'s Janet Maslin scoffed that *Cool World*'s "scenes combining live and animated action never match the caliber of 'Who Framed Roger Rabbit.'" Bakshi himself encouraged such comparisons when, in a *Times* profile, he credited Zemeckis's success for compelling him to return to the big screen after a mid-1980s hiatus in which he took up the brush. "'Roger Rabbit' had come out," he told the reporter Jamie Diamond, "animation was hot. I made 1,500 bucks in 10 years of painting; I thought it would be nice to pick up a piece of change. So I called my lawyer, who was still speaking to me because no one ever leaves Hollywood, and asked him where I should go to sell a movie."

The noirish *Cool World* opens in Las Vegas 1945 (Roger gets framed, by comparison, in 1947). From there, the animated mad scientist Doc Whiskers (voiced by Maurice LaMarche) whisks the unassuming World War II vet Frank Harris (Brad Pitt) into the movie's eponymous cartoon universe. That universe is home to a motley crew of so-called doodles, including the curvaceous, Jessica Rabbit–like Holli Would (voiced, then embodied, by Kim Basinger), a cartoon who dreams of becoming human—or "noid," in this universe's parlance. In *Cool World*, "the possibility of mingling those worlds, of joining real and animated space, of hybridizing, is presented as an act rife with potential calamity" (Telotte, *Animating Space* 181). Holli can only achieve her dream by bedding a human, but Cool World's oldest and only law stipulates that "noids do not have sex with doodles." Frank, involved in his own strictly second-base relationship with the doodle Lonette (voiced by Candi Milo), keeps tabs on Holli to make sure that she too remains chaste; "There'll be no crossovers while I'm around," he promises. But indeed there will be: In an improbable, or at least inexplicable, twist, Holli pulls Cool World's creator, the comics artist Jack Deebs (Gabriel Byrne), from modern-day Las Vegas, where he's serving time for murder; they go to bed, Holli goes live, and Cool World begins to collapse into the real world.

The threat of miscegenation between live-action and animated characters stretches at least as far back as Donald's lusty pursuit of those live girls on the beach in *The Three Caballeros* (1944), "suggesting the sort of impossible sexual involvement that disturbed some viewers expecting the usual Disney fare and which precipitated several protesting reviews" (Telotte, *Animating Space* 146)—among which we might number Nick Grinde's pointed "So what?" *Roger Rabbit* tamps that threat down into subtext, both in Jessica and Marvin Acme's patty-cake dalliance and in Jessica's fitful flirtation with Eddie Valiant. But Bakshi (*Fritz the Cat*'s owner, after all) elevates subtext to obsession: *Cool World*'s narrative arc rises and falls in hot pursuit of live-action animated sex. But if *Cool World* is more obviously turned on by this prospect than is *Roger Rabbit*, it's also more puritanical about the possibility. After Holli transforms from doodle to noid—bringing a slew of cartoon characters with her to a live-action, if still animated, Vegas (in the only sequence that approaches Zemeckis's madcap *Rabbit*)—Frank and a conveniently repentant Jack team up to send her back to Cool World. Jack succeeds while Frank dies trying; Frank's partner, Nails (voiced by Charlie Adler), brings Frank's body back to Cool World, where he's miraculously reborn as a doodle (as Stephen Hunter said, gibberish). "Oh, Nails, he's alive," Lonette coos as Frank assumes illustrated form, "and he's gorgeous too." A negligee-clad Lonette shoos Nails from the room and turns out the light, assuring the animated Frank that they can "stop pretending now." Holli, meanwhile, gets reluctantly reanimated—trapped in a comic book with a newly cartoon Jack ("pencil dick," she mutters, and not for the first time). In the film's closing moments, *Cool World* maintains a strict separation of noid and toon. There'll be no crossovers, ultimately, while Bakshi's around.

HOLLYROCK

Roger Rabbit's next most natural successor did not, in fact, much resemble *Roger Rabbit*. Dating back to the Stone Age of 1994, Brian Levant's blockbusting *The Flintstones*—the fifth highest grossing film worldwide that year—was produced, like *Roger Rabbit* before it and like *Casper* after it, by Steven Spielberg, who'd just topped the previous year's box office with *Jurassic Park* (chief among Sito's Gettysburgs). That flick and *The Flintstones* share a surprising amount of DNA—*Jurassic Park*'s extracted from ambered mosquitos, *The Flintstones*' from the amber hue of Golden Age cartoons. Spielberg explicitly connects the films in the later *Casper*'s press kit, lauding the producer Colin Wilson for his effects work on both *Jurassic Park* and *The Flintstones* (and *Roger Rabbit*, to boot; Universal Pictures 2). Tellingly, Wilson's effects, in both *Jurassic Park*'s wildlife and *The Flintstones*' fauna, flattens the animated/live-action divide. When we first see the Flintstones' lavender lap-dogasaurus Dino flanking the family's saber-toothed Baby Puss, he (and the big cat) are CG. When Dino pops his head up in the next scene to get a better view of a drive-in movie (*Tar Wars*), his noggin belongs to an actual animatronic puppet—recalling *Jurassic Park*'s sometimes CG, sometimes material *T. rex*. In both Bedrock and Jurassic Park—miles away from the bifurcated Cool World—animation and live action cross over and over and over.

The Flintstones pays homage to its nearby ancestor: Bedrock's town square includes a playground whose entrance is arced by a "Jurassic Park" sign, bony *T. rex* logo and all. But if this wink fossilizes a kinship between the two films, it also signals their evolutionary distance. Unlike *Jurassic Park*, *The Flintstones* domesticates animation. *Jurassic Park*'s animatronic and CG creations wreak Harryhausenesque havoc; *The Flintstones*' do the dishes. During the film's opening, Levant's camera descends into a valley outside Bedrock where two CG dinosaurs race through a river—but only after we've seen a computer-animated pterodactyl ferrying live-action passengers on its back ("And on your left, you'll be able to see the Grand Canyon—in about fifteen million years"). *The Flintstones'* dinosaurs can always be tamed and, in this instance, even made commercial (airliner or otherwise). The film centers this taming or domestication by borrowing its source material's conceit: that the Flintstones' world is essentially our own, a Neanderthal *Honeymooners*—or, in 1994, *Married . . . with Children* (Levant directed one episode of the series). Bedrock's town square also includes a "TOY-S-AURUS" and a "RocDonald's" ("over 19 dozen sold"). And a title card at the very end of the film features prehistoric trams under the encouragement, "WHEN IN HOLLYROCK VISIT UNIVERSHELL STUDIOS"—an affirmation that audiences can experience what *The Washington Post*'s Jane Horwitz unkindly calls the film's "amusement park ambiance" in real life too ("Family Filmgoer: 'Flintstones').

The Flintstones set a bedrock foundation for decades of live-action Saturday-morning remakes that adopted computer animation as a pet and, in some cases, as a familial relation. These remakes integrated animation into the newly live-action worlds of *The Adventures of Rocky & Bullwinkle* (2000); *Scooby-Doo* and *Scooby-Doo 2: Monsters Unleashed* (2004); *Garfield* and *Garfield: A Tale of Two Kitties* (2006); *Alvin and the Chipmunks, Alvin and the Chipmunks: The Squeakquel* (2009), *Alvin and the Chipmunks: Chipwrecked* (2011), and *Alvin and the Chipmunks: The Road Chip* (2015); *Yogi Bear* (2010); *The Smurfs* (2011) and *The Smurfs 2* (2013); *Woody Woodpecker* (2017); and *Tom and Jerry* (2021). Such titles—critically reviled, more often than not, for the same cash-in spirit that had led Morgenstern to ding *Casper* as an "infomercial"—led to CG's growing acceptance in the late 1990s and early 2000s, alongside more seemingly reputable hybrid productions like *Star Wars: Episode One—The Phantom Menace* (1999), *Harry Potter and the Sorcerer's Stone* (2001), and *The Lord of the Rings: The Fellowship of the Ring* (2001) and their sequels. Where *Harry Potter* and *The Lord of the Rings* arrived on screens pedigreed by British literature and Shakespearean-adjacent casts (Meikle 12–13), *The Flintstones* and its followers drew not only from midcentury cartoons but from the commercial breaks in between, where animated characters like Snap, Crackle, and Pop and Tony the Tiger encouraged real kids to eat their cereal (the author Gary Wolfe cited such ads as inspiration for *Who Censored Roger Rabbit*, the 1981 novel that became Zemeckis's 1988 film [Anderson 2019]). In this sense, *The Flintstones* and its extended family reminded us of what we already knew: that animation was already squatting in our homes, on our kitchen counters or in our cabinets—and had been, maybe, since the beginning of time.

WHIPSTAFF MANOR

Brad Silberling's *Casper*, which floated into US multi-plexes over Memorial Day weekend of 1995 (exactly a year after *The Flintstones'* own release), imagined live action and animation on even friendlier terms. Silber-ling's film could, by many rights, claim to be *Roger Rabbit's* true spiritual successor; the adolescent ghost had, after all, come close to appearing in Zemeckis's film, emerging from Marvin Acme's grave in a sprawl-ing funeral sequence that was storyboarded but never shot (Korkis). When *Casper* rose again, this time from *Roger Rabbit's* plot, his movie debut hovered, much like Zemeckis's film, between animation's future and its past. Like Levant's *Flintstones*, Silberling's *Casper* was both throwback—exorcizing its subject from the comic book pages and chintzy TV series in which he'd been trapped for half a century before—and au courant, rounding him out by way of digital animation. But *Casper* also evolved beyond even *The Flintstones'* best supporting dinos, pre-senting a fully realized CG lead. In a three-star review of the film, Ebert contemplated "the coming age of comput-erized performances in the movies," comparing Casper and his ghostly uncles to none other than Jessica Rabbit, an apparent harbinger of characters created from "bits and bytes" ("Casper"). In the film's press kit, the effects artist Dennis Muren likewise called Casper "the first digital *performer* ever" (Universal Pictures 7). *The New York Times*'s Caryn James likened the film's "overwhelm[ing]" effects not only to *Roger Rabbit*'s but also to the computer-generated wizardry—some of the first of its kind—in Zemeckis's *Death Becomes Her*. *Casper*'s hero, she wrote, "isn't even a cartoon, but an amazingly life-like swirl of digital effects with a baby face and big blue eyes. . . . Even in an age of escalating special-effects wizardry, 'Casper' is astonishing." *Cinefantastique*'s Persons wrote that, in taking on *Casper*, "Silberling found himself confronted with not just any garden-variety fantasy film, but a ground-breaking production that melded live-action actors with computer generated performers to an extent never before attempted"—some four hundred digital-effects shots to *Jurassic Park*'s fifty-something. The film was, per Persons, "a CGI blast from '50s animation past" that looked very much like and unlike *Roger Rabbit*.

While Casper originated from the same Golden Age of animation as Roger and his cohort, Silberling's film also showed just how quickly *Roger Rabbit*'s combination of cartoons and live actors had grown long in the tooth. The *Casper* producer Colin Wilson, who worked as an associate editor on Zemeckis's film, told *The Virginian-Pilot*, "We didn't want the film to be similar to 'Roger Rabbit.' We didn't want it to be flat" (Vincent). If *Roger Rabbit* was "ink-paint" (Wilson's phrase), *Casper* was "transparent" and "3-D" (Vincent). Whatever the film's considerable technical accomplishments, *Roger Rabbit* still took its cue from the live-action animated mash-ups of the mid-twentieth century; *Casper* peeked at the hybrid aesthetic that would come to dominate the twenty-first. The film's press kit stresses *Casper's* "ground-breaking" nature: "Never before had such an intricate and extensive combination of live action and state-of-the-art full-motion computer-generated images been attempted" (Universal Pictures 7).

Given the weight (or weightlessness?) of *Casper's* groundbreaking CG, the film's first line of dialogue— "OK, one picture and we're history"—could well have come from its director's lips. Instead, it's uttered by a young boy peering through a rusted gate, Polaroid camera in hand (a Spectra—boo!). At some distance sits Whipstaff Manor, the dilapidated New England mansion in which the boy and his friend hope to collect photographic evidence of their mettle. When Casper himself offers to help, however, taking the Polaroid camera into his translucent hands, the boys bolt for the door, screaming. Ghostly CG whisps coalesce into the film's title, obscuring the resulting photograph of the boys' horrified faces after it falls to the floor—out with the analog, in with the digital.

Yet if the specter of CG proves frightful in the film's opening, digital animation quickly gets friendlier. When a lonely Casper catches a news segment about the "paranormal therapist" Dr. James Harvey (Bill Pullman) and his teenage daughter, Kat (Christina Ricci), he conspires to bring the latter to Whipstaff by channeling the same segment to the mansion's recent inheritor, the bratty heiress Carrigan Crittenden (Cathy Moriarty). Crittenden hires the pair to exorcize the Manor, and when they arrive, Casper's all aflutter about Kat: "It's her, she's here, she's in my house. I did it! What if she likes me? What if she doesn't?" (In case *Casper*'s stakes weren't as transparent as its eponymous apparition, Silberling sets the film in a town called Friendship.) Kat faints when she first meets Casper, but she comes to, and comes around, soon enough. He makes her breakfast as she quizzes him about his composition ("What are you made of? . . . So, can you go invisible? . . . Can you hurt me? . . . Can I hurt you?"), culminating in Casper placing his palm against and then through Kat's, all while a haunting piano refrain swells on the soundtrack. This is the special friendship that Casper—and *Casper*—is after: between the living and the undead, between live action and digital animation.

After Kat first encounters Casper, she describes him to her father as a "real live ghost," a seeming contradiction in terms that, like the film at large, draws life and death (and, in turn, live action and digital animation) into ever-closer accord. At one point in the film, both Harvey and Critten-den turn into cartoonish CG spirits; at another, Casper becomes a real live boy (played by the 1990s heartthrob Devon Sawa) and shares a dance—and a kiss—with Kat. When he reverts to his ghost form, he joins hands with Harvey and Kat, dancing to the ubiquitous *Casper* theme song, signaling the start of a beautiful friendship.

LOONEY TUNE LAND

Whereas Casper revels in a series of ghastly live-action animated crossings-over, Joe Pytka's *Space Jam*, released a year and a half later, tips off from an initially more familiar crossover (the name, not incidentally, for one of basketball's most famous fake-outs). The film's first trailer promises in bombastic voice-over that "when the world's greatest athlete, Michael Jordan, teams up with the world's best loved cartoon character, Bugs Bunny, you won't believe your eyes." Where Roger Rabbit offered unheard-of meetings between toon icons (Donald and Daffy on the same stage!), *Space Jam* offered an unbeliev-able meet-up between live-action and animated icons—unprecedented, that is, except for the early 1990s Nike ads featuring Bugs, Marvin the Martian, and Jordan that had inspired the film in the first place. Indeed, in its team-up,

those ads and *Space Jam* followed an even earlier precedent, recasting the starry duets of midcentury mixed
pics (Gene and Jerry! Doris and Bugs! Esther and Tom
and Jerry!) with an athlete instead and drawing out that
match-up to a full four quarters. Choreographing Warner
Bros.' bunny alongside a Bull (one who would face his
own "last dance" in the season after *Space Jam*'s release)
was nothing new—a "novelty" rather than an "innovation," to borrow Paul Wells's distinction (182). Thus, the
Space Jam trailer's closing claim that "you've never seen
anything like it" rings a little false, especially given the
image on-screen: Bugs smooching Jordan just like Roger
locked lips with Eddie in *Roger Rabbit*.

But *Space Jam*'s playbook *did* differ from earlier live-
action animated films' in one important respect: Pytka
and his team—including several *Roger Rabbit* alums, like
Jones and Smith—added digital animators to their bench.
Even while *Space Jam* looks, at first blush, a lot like *Roger
Rabbit* (or *Cool World*), and less like *Casper*, the film more
pointedly literalizes a growing indistinction between
live action, 2D animation, and CG. When the *Space Jam*
trailer declares that "you won't believe your eyes," we
see Jordan, en route to his first meeting with Bugs, flying
through a digitally animated underground tunnel; what's
unbelievable is the sight of the athlete bouncing against
and breaking through a CG rendering of the 2D Warner

Bros. logo (encircled by those famous red rings) into Looney Tune Land. *Space Jam* didn't just combine live action and cel animation, as *Roger Rabbit* had done, but live action, cel animation, and innovative CG.

In a November 1996 *New York Times* feature on *Space Jam*, the producer Ivan Reitman praises Kelly's *Anchors Aweigh* scene as "very charming" but argues that "today's audiences needed a step forward in visual splendor" (Jackson). *Space Jam*'s makers achieved that splendor by combining green-screened live-action footage with separate cel animation into enough "digital information" to fill "a 10,000-square-foot warehouse" (Jackson). "People who use digital technology in the future, who use mixed media or combine live-action and traditional animation," Jones says, "will use 'Space Jam' as a goal. They won't use 'Roger Rabbit.' 'Roger Rabbit' used to be there. Now it's 'Space Jam'" (Jackson). The "Tech Notes" on *Space Jam*'s original website likewise align the film with its live-action animated ancestors (not just *Roger Rabbit* but the Alice comedies, *Anchors Aweigh*, and *Mary Poppins*), at the same time breaking decisively for the future: "Almost all the advances seen on the screen are due to the amazingly rapid progress in the application of computers to the field of animation—in fact, to virtually every aspect of *Space Jam*" (*Space Jam*, "Tech Notes"). Consider a crowd scene populated by "traditional all animated characters, 3-D animated characters and a crowd of actual people wearing masks," which was "computer scanned and then . . . manipulated to create a 'semi-animated' look that bridged the two worlds of live action and animation" (*Space Jam*, "Production Notes"). Or take a courtside scene that includes "a CGI floor; 2-dimensional chairs; digitalized computer shading and 'environment,' including smoke, haze and light; a live-action crowd; and a real ball and net, all combined into a single image on the screen" (*Space Jam*, "Production Notes"). It is a "single image" or—per *The Times*—"a seamless coexistence of the real, the virtual and the animated" (Jackson) that is less bifurcated, by far, than *Cool World* or even *Roger Rabbit*.

Even if *Space Jam*'s seams look more frayed now than they did in 1996, the film's combination of live action, 2D, and CG remains a monumental team-building exercise. From some of *Space Jam*'s very first frames, Pytka plays fast and loose with live action and animation, as in one seemingly "unbroken camera movement" (*Space Jam*, "Production Notes") that takes us from a real-world Chicago press conference to outer space, where we survey the CG Moron Mountain, home to the film's villains, the hapless Nerdlucks, themselves rendered in 2D. As in Jordan's overlong dunk at the film's end, this shot uses non- (or not-yet-) traditional CG to bridge live action and "traditional" animation. Elsewhere, CG *subs in* for live action, much as 2D once did in *Anchors Aweigh* (when Kelly exits the foreground of the frame in live action and reappears, in the distance, as a right-sized cartoon) or as stop-motion did in Harryhausen's films (with live actors replaced by approximate models in distant dinosaur attacks). A live-action golf ball becomes CG once Bugs assumes control of it with a magnet, drawing Jordan to the hole through which he'll tumble to Looney Tune Land. Once there, Porky Pig empties a locker of 2D basketballs, but the ball passed between the Tunes is rendered in 3D CG. This slippage extends to Jordan's body; when a doctored Daffy checks him out with an otoscope, his ear canal appears in grotesque, *Ren and Stimpy*–ish 2D (a sign, maybe, that the animation was in him all along). In another early scene, a digitally animated Jordan himself *becomes* a basketball, "stretched, squashed, and . . . wadded up" (*Space Jam*, "Tech Notes") by the rival 2D b-ballers, the Monstars. As Jordan goes looney, so does the baseline or endline separating live action from both 2D and 3D animation. Through such sleights and stretches of hand, *Space Jam* drafts a third player—"the virtual," the CG—into live action and 2D's previously one-on-one match-up.

HOLLYWOOD

The Flintstones, *Casper*, and *Space Jam* prefaced a decade (or two) in which Hollywood regularly retooled Saturday-morning cartoons for the newly digital cinema. Those remakes eventually, and perhaps naturally, converged on Hollywood itself, in the Los Angeles–set *Alvin and the Chipmunks*. *Alvin* took its inspiration from Ross Bagdasarian Sr.'s diminutive pop trio, whose hit Christmas single "The Chipmunk Song (Don't Be Late)" debuted in 1958 and launched Alvin, Simon, and Theodore onto comic book pages and TV airwaves in the decades thereafter. (Zemeckis himself was attached to an *Alvin* film in the early 1990s, after one proposed *Roger Rabbit* sequel fell apart.) *Alvin and the Chipmunks'* 2007 revival—followed by three squeakquels, each as critically dismissed and commercially robust as the last—hits many of the cartoon remake cycle's major notes. First, Alvin and his brothers are modeled (as are Rocky, Bullwinkle, Scooby, Garfield, Yogi, Woody, and Tom and Jerry) on living creatures, great and (often) small—very much *unlike* the animated creations more obviously associated with the digital Gettysburgs: *The Phantom Menace*'s Jar Jar Binks and *The Fellowship of the Ring*'s Gollum, fantastic characters whose connection to their respective human counterparts (Ahmed Best and Andy

Serkis) nevertheless remains clear. In this respect, Alvin and company are both *less* natural, in their lack of connection to any such counterpart, and *more* so, in that they're based on real animals.

This natural fact (to recall "Opposites Attract") connects to the cartoon remake cycle's second distinguishing feature: a tendency to *naturalize* its animated leads, cartoonish though they may be. In *Rocky and Bullwinkle*, the FBI agent Karen Sympathy (Piper Perabo) at one point tries to rescue the titular squirrel and moose by claiming that she needs them as part of her work for the "Committee for Animated Wildlife Preservation." In *Garfield*, Nermal is played by an actual Siamese cat, inviting equivalence between her and the CG orange tabby. *Alvin and the Chipmunks*, like *Yogi Bear* and *Woody the Woodpecker*, opens outdoors—with majestic establishing shots of a forest—before settling on the chipmunks, unclothed, stuffing nuts into a fir tree. Only the chipmunks' oversize heads, atop otherwise realistically textured bodies, disturb the image's naturalism—that and the fact that they're singing Daniel Powter's 2005 pop hit "Bad Day" to pass the time. Alvin complains that he's "sick of struggling for survival, competing with gophers and earthworms and that loser sparrow who always takes [his] nuts"; luckily for Alvin, a trio of farmers fell the tree, delivering it to an office building in the city where it's adorned with Christmas lights, in a wink to the Chipmunks' original yuletide packaging. When the Chipmunks cross paths with the aspiring songwriter and part-time adman Dave Seville (Jason Lee)—who initially calls them "creepy" and "unnatural"—he has to domesticate them, starting by knitting their already-iconic red, blue, and green jumpers. Midway through *Yogi Bear*, we similarly see the titular character (voiced by Dan Aykroyd) throw his iconic hat and tie aside after Ranger Smith (Tom Cavanagh) tells him that he's *not* smarter than an average bear; Yogi explains to Boo Boo (voiced by Justin Timberlake) that he's going to "forage for food in the wild," to "catch some fish with [his] paws." Alvin and Yogi are just a jumper or tie away from wild—a point that *Yogi Bear* (the film) stresses by having another park ranger (Anna Faris) remark that talking brown bears "are so rare" and that the *Woody Woodpecker* film underscores by identifying *its* eponymous rascal as a pileated red-crowned woodpecker, another rare species, worth some half a million dollars on the black market. As if to further plead their case, Woody and the Chipmunks encounter decidedly *unnatural*, google-eyed, inanimate versions of themselves, the former in a decoy laid by money-grubbing hunters, the latter in (yet again google- and dead-eyed) stuffed animals that *they* use as decoys to fool a money-grubbing record producer (played by David Cross) in *Alvin and the Chipmunks'* finale.

The Chipmunks' trickery signals the live-action cartoon remake's third major tasting note: product placement. Alvin, Simon, and Theodore's decoys are cheap tie-in toys that the record producer manufactures after the trio become famous; surely the film's own tie-in merchandise underwent a more thorough vetting process. Indeed, in one uncanny sense, 3D cartoon remakes bring their central characters more in line with the polyester plush dolls and plastic figurines that they inspired in the first place; their rounded-out forms may, in that way, look less *unnatural* than we might think. But these remakes go even more explicitly commercial elsewhere, in product placement so shameless that Common Sense Media—a site that provides content info on family films—notes the "surprisingly mild" consumerism in a movie like *Yogi Bear*—limited to stealth ads for just "a few cars" ("Yogi Bear"). Common Sense cites *Alvin* for "several scenes involv[ing] the chipmunks watching *SpongeBob SquarePants*" (the film's director, Tim Hill, was a writer on the show), "eating/heating Van's waffles," and spotlighting brands like Hummer, Porsche, Apple, Bose, and Tabasco ("Alvin and the Chipmunks")—though the site curiously makes no mention of UTZ, whose cheese balls pop up so often in Dave's kitchen that they should get their own credit. If this product placement serves as a crass reminder of the adaptations' *own* commercial impetuses, it also chips away at the fourth wall separating Alvin's world from ours. Product placement becomes another form of direct address in movies where characters frequently speak to audiences ("I know what you folks are thinking: Woody is a big, fat sellout!" the Woodpecker says at one point; "Don't you ever have anything to say?" he asks at another). These interjections—coupled with the product placement's more indirect address—yet again collapse the boundaries separating Woody's or Alvin's world from ours, in a manner quite different from *Anchors Aweigh*'s fantastic vertigo. More mundanely, we buy into these worlds so that we might buy UTZ or Bose or Van's in our own.

Appropriately, then, these films tend to end with a kind of product *integration*; Woody, Yogi, and Alvin and the Chipmunks all eventually come to some kind of accord with their live-action antagonists or (more often) deuter-agonists. Woody shacks up with the father and son whose house he'd been intent on destroying ("Just because I'm one of a kind doesn't mean I can't be part of a family too," he says); Yogi ends up drawing visitors to Jellystone Park, much to Ranger Smith's delight; and Alvin, Simon, and Theodore achieve international stardom with Dave's help—but, more importantly, get Dave to admit that they're all family along the way (the first squeakquel ends with that family expanding to include the Chipettes). The animated characters and their live-action counterparts achieve symbiosis; they cohabitate—they hang out and room together—all in longer leases and agreements than any we might find in the midcentury mixed pic. In these living arrangements, Alvin and the Chipmunks (and company) arguably set the foundation for some of the most successful hybrid buddy movies of the young twenty-first century: 2012's *Ted* and its 2015 sequel, 2019's *Detective Pikachu*, and 2020's *Sonic the Hedgehog* and its sequels.

ANDALASIA/MANHATTAN

A second chipmunk's furtive movements, in 2007's *Enchanted* (released the same year as the first *Alvin*), lead the way to the *other* most successful live-action animated movies of the 2010s and 2020s, movies that indistinguishably integrate live action and animation. *Enchanted* begins in the animated fairy-tale land of Andalasia but quickly sends its princess, Giselle (first voiced and then embodied by Amy Adams), through a magical well to a lively and live-action Times Square. When Pip the chipmunk follows after her, he morphs from a 2D, wisecracking sidekick (in the vein of *Mulan*'s Mushu) into a 3D, photorealistic chipmunk—no oversize head here—without the gift of gab, in line with the film's fish-out-of-water conceit. The film cements that conceit with a subsequent scene where Giselle, crashing at a divorce lawyer's apartment after he finds her in the middle of the street, opens the apartment's window and sings a melody not unlike Snow White's 1937 well-wishing. Pigeons, cockroaches, flies, and rats come to Giselle's call, helping her clean the apartment in another *Snow White* riff, this one of that film's "Happy Working Song." Elsewhere, Pip can only communicate to Prince Edward (James Marsden), who's come to New York looking for Giselle, in charades.

While the joke in this scene seems to be about what happens when Disney characters stop being 2D and start getting real, its punch line is a doozy: *Enchanted* was released just one year before *Iron Man* (2008), two years before Disney acquired Marvel, and three years before Disney released *Alice in Wonderland* (2010), the first film in an ongoing live-action remake cycle (and a film that fittingly features a portal from a live-action world to a more animated land). Disney's remakes of *The Jungle Book* (2016), *The Lion King* (2019), and *The Lady and the Tramp* (2019) would follow in the decade after, each featuring its own photo-realistic animals behaving like their animated forebears—who, unlike in *Enchanted*, are nowhere to be seen. Disney went so far as to market *The Lion King*, bereft of any human character, as a live-action film, even while (with the possible exception of a few establishing shots), everything is animated. As Chris Holliday observes, *The Lion King*'s "sophisticated developments in animated technology—from VR and tracking systems to its broader treatment of the virtual backlot—[had] the paradoxical effect of helping to secure its identity as *more* live action."

Viewed from this angle, *Enchanted* looks less like a parody and more like a plan. The live-action environments where cartoons find happy homes in *Alvin* and its related remakes give way, in Disney's retreads, to all-encompassing animated worlds surely in the same orbit as *Thor: Ragnarok* (2017) and the galaxies far, far, away (in another Disney universe). Disney's remakes draw on the hybrid grammar of contemporary blockbusters at the same time that they draw Disney into closer accord *with* those hybrid blockbusters. Consider how Sean Bailey, Walt Disney Studios' president of motion picture production, describes developing the live-action *Maleficent* in a 2017 *Vulture* interview: "We thought if Iron Man and Thor and Captain America are Marvel superheroes, then maybe Alice, Cinderella, Mowgli, and Belle are our superheroes, and Cruella and Maleficent are our supervillains" (Taylor). Bailey's dream came true: When Disney released the live-action *Cruella* (a *Maleficent*-like *101 Dalmatians* prequel) in 2021, Twitter's denizens dubbed the film "Disney's *Joker*" (Bentz). When Gal Gadot confirmed her casting as the Evil Queen in Disney's live-action *Snow White* (2025), she did so with an Instagram post celebrating fan-art mash-ups of the Queen and Wonder Woman, the role for which she's best known. How quaint that, in the early days of the Marvel and Lucasfilm deals, fans worried about the Disneyfication of the Avengers or Star Wars ("Looking forward to seeing what exciting new Star Wars adventures will be cooked up by the dream factory that brought us Mars Needs Moms!" tweeted *Family Guy* creator Seth MacFarlane; qtd. in Itzkoff). If anything, Disney became more Marvelous or Lucasfilmic. *The Lion King* remake's Simba may look uncanny when set against his expressionistic 2D predecessor, but he could easily stand as Guardian alongside Rocket Raccoon. In the Disney cinematic universe, live action and animation no longer dust it up as they do in Harryhausen's fantasies, no longer tango together as they do in *Anchors Aweigh*, no longer cohabitate as they do in *Alvin*; they can't, because they're one and the same.

THE NORTH POLE

In 1998, just before the turn of the millennium, Roger Rabbit briefly reappeared above ground, starring in a ten-second screen test—seen by a select few Disney execs and directed by the animator Eric Goldberg—in which a 3D, CG Roger Rabbit pulls himself out of a top hat and belts "Gotta Dance" as he taps and hops his way onto an unnamed private eye's desk (the test eventually made its way to YouTube). In a 2010 *Cartoon Brew* post, Goldberg recalls the scene's genesis: "Why don't we see if we can do Roger himself in CG? If we can animate something as fluid and eminently squashy-stretchy as Roger Rabbit, then we can animate anything in CG" (Beck). The director stipulates that "whether we would use the technique or not in the sequel, it was to prove that we could do Disney quality animation in CG, which no one had ever attempted before" (Beck). And to Goldberg, at least, "Roger was tracked perfectly, the same way the dinosaurs in *Jurassic Park* were tracked perfectly" (Beck). *Roger Rabbit*'s sequel never materialized—and, as Ross Anderson points out, Disney would go on to acquire Pixar (which *was* doing "Disney quality animation in CG") shortly thereafter, in 2006 (176–77).

In 2002, as *Roger Rabbit*'s follow-up continued to roast in development hell, Zemeckis himself retired to chillier climes, mounting a digitally animated adaptation of Chris Van Allsburg's yuletide picture book *The Polar Express*. In *The Polar Express* (2004), Zemeckis employed motion-capture technology that allowed Tom Hanks to play every major role in the movie, from the skeptical boy who boards the eponymous train to the train's conductor to St. Nick himself. The actor's "movement and facial expressions," explains the *Washington Post* critic Jane Horwitz (seen earlier disowning *The Flintstones*), "were mapped into a computer program, then wedded to virtual costumes, sets and backgrounds. The result has a you-are-there three-dimensionality, but little emotional pull and a presumably unintentional creepiness" ("Family Filmgoer"). While Horwitz recoiled at *The Polar Express*'s digital miens, "which look neither human nor animated" ("Family Filmgoer"), Roger Ebert was charmed by their indeterminacy: "The characters in 'The Polar Express' don't look real, but they don't look unreal, either; they have a kind of simplified and underlined reality that makes them visually magnetic" ("Polar Express"). In a four-star review, he exalted the look of Zemeckis's adaptation as "extraordinary," a "cross between live action and Van Allsburg's artwork" ("Polar Express"). Ebert goes on to note that while Zemeckis's *Roger Rabbit* "juxtaposed live action with animation, this time [he] merges them" ("Polar Express"). Zemeckis would continue merging live action with animation, in both the motion-capture epic *Beowulf* (2007) and the Disney-backed *A Christmas Carol* (2009). "As much as [*Roger Rabbit*] spectacularized hybridity," writes Bob Rehak, "Zemeckis's more recent productions have tried to sublimate it" (172).

The director's own Disney live-action remake, of 1940's *Pinocchio*, debuted in 2021. In a strange twist, Zemeckis's film doesn't end with Pinocchio's typical transformation into a real boy; instead, a CG Pinocchio, still wooden, walks hand in hand with Geppetto (Tom Hanks) into the distance. As they disappear, a CG Jiminy Cricket (voiced by Joseph Gordon-Levitt) addresses the audience directly: "Since then, many stories have been told about [Pinocchio]. People say he was transformed into an honest to goodness real boy. Did that actually happen?" Pinocchio's spindled leg momentarily takes on the heft of human (but still digitally animated) flesh. "Who knows?" asks Jiminy. "But I do know one thing for sure: In his heart, Pinocchio is as real as any real boy could ever be." Zemeckis pointedly employs Pinocchio to render the line between animation and live action irrelevant. No further questions, he says, at this time—a moment when Disney was rapidly erasing said line via the very platform on which *Pinocchio* debuted: Disney+. It is to that platform, and its live-action animated mergers, that we turn next.

3

SYNERGY (1941–2022)

Nearly thirty-five years after Roger Rabbit's blockbuster debut, he at last returned to feature films in another Los Angeles–set live-action animated mystery, 2022's *Chip 'n Dale: Rescue Rangers*. In *Chip 'n Dale*, the eponymous stars of the late-1980s animated series (voiced, this time around, by John Mulaney and Andy Sandberg) reunite after a decades-long falling out when their former costar, Monterey Jack (voiced by Eric Bana), goes missing. With the help of officer Ellie (Kiki Layne), their human foil, the chipmunks quickly uncover a wide-ranging bootleg operation run by wiseguy Sweet Pete (voiced by Will Arnett), whose means of persuasion include a jar of Dip pulled from *Roger Rabbit*'s shelf. Pete, a middle-aged version of Disney's Boy Who Wouldn't Grow Up, kidnaps toons, only to reassemble and resell them in tawdry knockoffs like *Beauty and the Cursed Dog Man* (an offbeat *Beauty and the Beast*), *Jasper the Dead Ghost Kid* (an off-brand *Casper*), and *Spaghetti Dogs* (an off-leash *Lady and the Tramp*). In *Chip 'n Dale*, as in *Roger Rabbit*, animated characters from different studios, series, and eras mingle indiscriminately. One early 1990s flashback finds the Rescue Rangers partying alongside the Three Little Pigs (from Disney's 1933 short), Paula Abdul and MC Skat Kat (from the "Opposites Attract" video), and none other than Roger himself. "We were livin' the dream," Dale reflects in voice-over, "high on the hog, all night long dancing the Roger Rabbit—*with* Roger Rabbit!" We see Roger (again voiced by Charles Fleischer) exclaim, "Woo, boy, what a party!" as Abdul and Skat Kat spin Heavy D and the Boyz's "Now That We Found Love"—an implied happy ending, perhaps, for the former opposites.

Indeed, in *Chip 'n Dale*, live action and animation have already found love: An even earlier flashback shows young Chip and Dale attending a school populated by both humans and toons. In a shot that recalls *Roger Rabbit*'s opening tour of Maroon Studios' backlot, we watch real live kids stream into Unionville Elementary, 1982, alongside tons of toons: an animated boy wearing a live-action backpack; a hoodied goat ("Betty, you're not Donald Duck!" admonishes a human administrator. "Put some pants on please!"); and a car toon dropping off a couple of bumper cars before Dale hops off an actual school bus. That indistinction extends to present-day Los Angeles, where, for instance, Chip works at an insurance agency alongside both humans and a CG bull and frog or where Ellie's boss at the police station, Captain Putty (voiced by J. K. Simmons), just happens to be clay-animated. Even if we're wont to distinguish between live action and animation, it's workaday—unremarkable. A pair of scenes set at a fan convention lean into this hal-lucinogenic congruence, featuring real people dressed as toons (a Pickle Rick from *Rick and Morty*, a George Jetson, a LEGO fella, a Miguel from *Coco*, a Moana from *Moana*); toons dressed like real people (CG mice styled as Star Wars' Princess Leia and Kylo Ren, a young 2D woman in a *Ghostbusters* sweatshirt and matching head-band); people dressed as cartoonish people (a Pee Wee Herman, a crew member from the partially stop-motion *Life Aquatic with Steve Zissou*); and people dressed as characters who've been both flat and flesh (e.g., *Beauty and the Beast*'s Belle, animated by Disney in 1991 but lively in a 2017 remake). Meanwhile, the formerly 2D Dale even gets "CGI surgery" to rejuvenate his career, an unsubtle nod to another rodent's more photo-realistic big-screen makeover; Pete at one point admits that he was "always more of an *Alvin and the Chipmunks* person." At the convention, a photo-realistic CG Baloo the bear, from Disney's 2016 remake of 1967's animated *Jungle Book*, fronts a band backed by a 2D hound dog saxophonist and a live-action keyboardist. In Chip and Dale's world, live action and animation play exceedingly well—and increasingly fast and loose—together.

Chip 'n Dale was just one of several films in and around the 2020s that not only integrated live action and animation but *synergized* live action and animated properties. Nearly a hundred years after Disney's Little Alice disappeared down the rabbit hole, movies like *Ready Player One* (2018) and *Space Jam: A New Legacy* (2021) imagined their own intertextual wonderlands whose live-action and animated mergers were more corporate than corporeal; both films' monster mash-ups include humans and toons from Warner Bros. properties like *The Shining*, Nightmare on Elm Street, Batman, and *The Iron Giant*.

After mingling within the film frame for a century, live action and animation began to mingle outside those frames too. No doubt, such combinations were motivated by a series of actual mergers and acquisitions that vastly expanded those studios' content libraries and made for some unexpected bedfellows—Disney bought Marvel in 2009, Lucasfilm in 2012, and Fox in 2019; WarnerMedia combined with Discovery Inc. in 2022; Paramount Global agreed to combine with Skydance Media in 2024. But, as *Roger Rabbit* had attested in 1988, sometimes the most unlikely of bedfellows made for the best sex. Zemeckis's film, after all, mashed up characters from not only different studios but two very different sides of the *same* studio: the kiddish Disney and its more grown-up Touchstone, the label behind, or in front of, titles like *Splash* (1984), *The Color of Money* (1986), and *Good Morning, Vietnam* (1987). The twenty-first century's mergers fetishized this odd coupling, such that, in *A New Legacy*, *A Clockwork Orange*'s (1971) Droogs appeared courtside next to a cartoonish flying monkey from *The Wizard of Oz* (1939). In these movies, the increasingly unremarkable meeting of live-action and animated bodies served as mere pretense for more extraordinary, orgiastic combinations of live-action and animated intellectual property (IP). The newly amalgamated Disney, Warner, and Paramount reveled in their carnivalesque, merger-driven mash-ups.

Hence why, rather than *Roger Rabbit*'s live-action animated will-they-won't-they, *Chip 'n Dale*'s drama stems from the threat of IP theft. Pete and his henchman—a Coca-Cola polar bear and a dead-eyed CG Viking who wouldn't look out of place in Robert Zemeckis's *The Polar Express* (2004) or *Beowulf* (2007)—at one point infiltrate Fan Con in pursuit of Chip and Dale. They chase the pair through throngs of characters drawn from different properties: *Beauty and the Beast*'s Lumiere, *My Little Pony: Friendship Is Magic*'s Mane Six, Marvel's Tigra and the Marvel Cinematic Universe's Ant-Man (Paul Rudd), and Ugly Sonic (voiced by Tim Robinson), an early, much-maligned version of the CG wiseass who eventually—and less toothily, more toothsomely—headlined 2020's *Sonic the Hedgehog*. Fan Con's fantasia stands in contrast to Pete's seedy headquarters, wallpapered with bits of dismembered toons: the Pink Panther's snout, Mickey's glove, Jimmy Neutron's hair—all fodder for his pirated flicks. Midway through the film, Chip only escapes that headquarters after Pete has sutured a Snoopyesque ear to his chipmunk head. And, during the film's climax, Pete himself mutates into a tempestuous combination of different characters, his body and voice an amalgam of (among others) *Rescue Rangers'* Fat Cat, *101 Dalmatians'* Cruella de Vil, *Teenage Mutant Ninja Turtles'* Shredder, *Wreck-It Ralph*'s Ralph, and *Jurassic Park*'s CG *T. rex*. Pete's monstrous operation represents the dark underbelly of Fan Con's up-and-up accord. Contrary to Pete's shadier remixing, Fan Con's more conventional blend of intellectual properties is copyright cleared and studio sanctioned—just like *Chip 'n Dale*'s own.

If *Chip 'n Dale* crested a wave of combination films that hastened the collapse between live action and animation off-screen as well as on-, that tsunamic shift had been building for decades. Looking back, *Chip 'n Dale* and company's intertextual hijinks emphasize just how often the live-action animated film depended on other kinds of combining. Recall that in *Hollywood Party* (1934), live action didn't just meet animation; Mickey Mouse met Jimmy Durante and, by extension, Laurel and Hardy and the Three Stooges, big-screen brands to rival his own. Gene Kelly and Jerry Mouse's scene in *Anchors Aweigh* wasn't just a dance between live action and animation but also a tango between two of MGM's biggest stars at the time (like Esther Williams later getting dangerous when wet with Tom and Jerry). And *Roger Rabbit* wasn't just revelatory for its feature-length negotiation between live action and animation but also for its aforementioned, unprecedented—and heavily negotiated—clash of stars from rival studios (with Daffy squaring off against Donald on piano and Bugs Bunny and Mickey skydiving together). Long before *Roger Rabbit*, Disney had experimented with combining its own live-action and animated IP alongside live action and animation, not only in the so-called combination films of the 1940s but also in the small-screen *Disneyland* and *Wonderful World of Disney*, as well the theme parks that those shows ostensibly promoted.

While *Chip 'n Dale* glanced back at the IP vertigo of yore, the film looked ahead to the future of live-action animated combinations. The *Rescue Rangers* reboot itself debuted on smaller screens, bypassing theaters to land on Disney+; *A New Legacy*, meanwhile, premiered on

Warner Bros.' HBO Max. On such streaming platforms—both cause and effect of their parent companies' mergers—live-action and animated properties sat side by side (and sometimes literally faded into one another, via autoplay). *A New Legacy*'s and *Ready Player One*'s IP mashups take place, not incidentally, in entirely digital worlds, with galaxies of content-specific planets (e.g., Game of Thrones and Harry Potter) that look as much like HBO Max's streaming hub at the time as they do like different theme-park lands. In such hubs, any lingering distinction between live action and animation narrowed, finally, to a vanishing point.

That vanishing point looked different from the one that Nick Grinde had imagined in *The Screen Writer*'s pages in 1946, where he considered the contours of live action and animation and what the former could do for the latter as a "story telling [*sic*] ingredient" (26). Midcentury Technicolor musicals and stop-motion creature features told one story about animation's can-do synchronicity through their carefully choreographed dances and duels; the cartoon reboots and remakes of the 1990s and early 2000s told another, about integrating computer animation into live action and making it feel natural, at home. *Chip 'n Dale* 'n *Ready Player One* 'n *A New Legacy* tell a different story altogether, not about live action's and animation's respective properties but about live action and animation *as properties*, intellectually speaking. That story stretches back to the time of Grinde's writing and runs parallel to those mid- to late twentieth- and early twenty-first-century pics; Disney yet again figures as a main character. The moral of the story? That the live-action animated film as we know it wasn't just encouraged by artistic and technological leaps but also by conglomeration. Any distinction between live-action and animation properties quickly dissipated as they drifted—really, streamed—through the tributaries of Disney's, Warner Bros.', and Paramount's undifferentiated content.

THE RELUCTANT DRAGON

The animated denizens singing "Smile Darn Ya Smile" at *Roger Rabbit*'s end, amid the wreckage of the wall once separating Los Angeles and Toontown, include none other than the Reluctant Dragon, star of Disney's 1941 package picture of the same name. *The Reluctant Dragon*, more than any other package picture that Disney produced in the 1940s, anticipates *Roger Rabbit*'s (then *Rescue Rangers'*) intermedial/intertextual mischief. The movie begins with a title card explaining, "This picture is made in answer to the many requests to show the backstage life of animated cartoons," suggesting that those cartoons are working and walking around in real life, a conceit borrowed from *You Ought to Be in Pictures* (1940) and fully realized in *Roger Rabbit. The Reluctant Dragon*'s producers append a winking postscript ("Any resemblance to a regular motion picture is purely coincidental"), recalling *other* disclaimers that distance film characters from their possible real-life inspirations—a move that *invites* comparison even while trying to deny it. Further confusing matters, the actor Robert Benchley plays himself, or some version thereof, who hopes to sell Kenneth Grahame's *The Reluctant Dragon* to Disney—"I mean the idea, for a movie," he says. Almost all of Disney's future live-action animated films, including *Song of the South, So Dear to My Heart, Mary Poppins, Bedknobs and Broomsticks*, and *Pete's Dragon*, were based on children's literature more specific than the public-domain fare the studio mined for its strictly animated features.

The Reluctant Dragon does culminate in a strict animated adaptation of Grahame's book, but only after showcasing a remarkably lenient blend of live action and animation. When Benchley strikes on his idea to sell *The Reluctant Dragon*—toppling over a float in his backyard pool—he burbles out a cascade of animated bubbles, and the rambling tour of Disney's studio he embarks on thereafter only further muddies the waters. There, he gets cartoonishly "shushed" by an Atomizer during a recording session; the Atomizer belongs to none other than Clarence Nash, the voice of Donald Duck, who's preparing to take the stage (and later teaches Benchley how to quack). At another recording session, for an animated short drawn from *Dumbo*, Benchley pops his collar after lightning and thunder descend on-screen, cleaving the boundary between cartoon and studio; the director, Alfred Werker, does the same, cutting indiscriminately between the short itself and the making of. Further on, Donald himself (after we've seen and heard Nash) looks up from his cel to tell Benchley how animation works; Bambi, in another cel, runs away after Benchley says he'd like to take the fawn home with him.

Again, live action and animation go both ways: When we tour the psychedelic "Rainbow Room" where Benchley eventually encounters Bambi, *Snow White*'s "Heigh-Ho" plays over the soundtrack, making the space cartoonish. In this room devoted to blending and mixing, live action and animation run together. But so too do the studio's titles: *Bambi, Dumbo, Snow White*. That is, the package film's pleasure stems as much from the *intertextual* collapse of different properties into one another as from the intermedial collapse of live action into animation. In the Rainbow Room and beyond, the blending of properties makes the blending of live action and animation all the more probable, if not permissible, and vice versa.

DISNEYLAND/*DISNEYLAND*

The package films in general (and *The Reluctant Dragon*'s studio setting in particular) imagine a physical proximity between live action and animation matched only by Disney's later theme-park forays. Disneyland packages together disparate live-action and/or animated properties (Indiana Jones, Chip 'n Dale, Star Wars, Toy Story) and allows visitors to rub shoulders, sometimes literally, with real, live cartoons—animatronic or costumed. In *Disneyland: The First 50 Magical Years*, a short film that began playing exclusively in Disneyland's Main Street Opera House in 2005 as part of the park's semicentennial celebration, Steve Martin rubs shoulders with Donald Duck. Martin narrates a history of Disneyland as the puckish duck interlopes, Forrest Gump–like, in historical footage; the park, it seems, has always been part animated. Martin goes on to stress that Disneyland "was created by the same artists who created Disney's animated films at the studio, and soon those storybook tales came to life at an orange grove in Anaheim. For the first time, we could step into those worlds and become a part of the adventure." As he says so, a shot of artists sketching an elephant for *Dumbo* (there's a similar scene in *The Reluctant Dragon*) crossfades into a shot of the animated Dumbo flying, which itself crossfades into a shot of a child riding Dumbo at Disneyland. A subsequent sequence crossfades from a shot of a cartoon Peter Pan flying high above cartoon London into archival footage of a woman riding Peter Pan's Flight into a shot of Martin riding a ship from Peter Pan's Flight through an entirely animated sky, bumping against a sky-bound ship helmed by a piratical Donald.

These chains of association make clear that live action and animation exist not in opposition to each other but on a spectrum—a spectrum along which you can travel in Disney's parks. Just two years after the *Magical* short's debut, visitors to Orlando's Walt Disney World could float alongside Donald in Epcot's newly rethemed Gran Fiesta Tour, a boat ride through a faux Mexico guided by none other than the Three Caballeros. The ride renders Donald and the Caballeros in both 2D, on screens as they move through postcard vistas of Mexican beaches, and 3D, as musical animatronics at the attraction's end; the riders, of course, supply most of the live action. The Mesoamerican pyramid that houses the Gran Fiesta Tour, meanwhile, sits in the middle of its own live-action animated spectrum: If riders exit to the right, they're less than ten minutes from Cosmic Rewind, a roller coaster based on the hybrid Guardians of the Galaxy franchise; if they exit to the left, they're two minutes from a Frozen boat ride in faux Norway, based on Disney's computer-animated behemoth. In either direction, they might pass by one of Epcot's Magic Shot spots—photo ops where, through Disney's magic app, guests find themselves with the park's cartoon Orange Bird mascot perched on their finger or *Encanto*'s CG Isabela posing next to them under an animated stream of pink flowers. Disney World is both live action and animated, right and left, inside and out.

This conflation dates all the way back to the original Disneyland's opening and the small-screen show(s) used to promote the theme park's textual and aesthetic crossovers. Walt Disney's televisual *Disneyland* premiered in 1954, just a year before the Anaheim park opened. The show's first episode, "The Disneyland Story," begins *Reluctant*ly, with a behind-the-scenes sweep of concurrent productions: *20,000 Leagues Under the Sea*'s Kirk Douglas and Peter Lorre sit for makeup; Disney artists sketch *Sleeping Beauty*'s Aurora as a live model twirls to "Once upon a Dream"; the "MUSIC DEPT" works on toonish sound effects, their strange instrumentation captured in canted angles. The episode's narrator teases that "something unusual is going on in the studio today, something that never happened before"—something that lies behind the doors of the "DISNEYLAND PLANS ROOM," where we join Disney and "this little fella here" (says Walt), Mickey, framed in a painting on the wall. "It's an old partnership," Disney reflects. "Mickey and I started out the first time many, many years ago. We've had a lot of our dreams come true. Now we want you to share with us our latest and greatest dream." Disney pivots to another, larger painting next to Mickey's: Disneyland, "seen from about two thousand feet in the air, and ten months away." Pencil in hand, Disney taps on another map, in close-up, to show viewers the "240 acres near the city of Anaheim in Southern California" where "we've begun to build Disneyland the place"; the map dissolves into several aerial shots of the actual land. Pencil still in hand, Walt strides over to a scale model of Disneyland's entrance, whose buildings the camera tracks past at eye level, making them (momentarily) indistinguishable from the real thing. The rest of the episode glimpses at future installments of the series that'll be tied to one of the park's themed lands— Davy Crockett stories connected to Frontierland, for instance, or a truncated version of *Alice in Wonderland* (1951) inspired by Fantasyland. As Disney explains at the premiere's outset, "Disneyland the place and Disneyland the TV show are all part of the same."

For J. P. Telotte, Disney's conflation of place and show promised viewers "a kind of hybrid [experience], wherein traditional boundaries became fluid or even disappeared, wherein one sort of text borrows from or depends on another" (*Disney TV* 76). For Telotte, *Disneyland* presented viewers with "a curious amalgam of different media, something that would draw on a variety of appeals—films, television, the amusement park, even traditional cartooning" (*Disney TV* 77). The show's unprecedented intertextual sprawl, I would add, also dissipated or disappeared the boundaries between live action and animation. Like Disney and Mickey, live action and animation are partners in this intro, trading hands throughout. Watch as our host taps a pencil—the animator's tool—to take us from the hand-drawn map to actual shots of Southern California; watch as he holds onto that pencil while moving from the map in the background to the model in the foreground. Abracadabra: Disney collapses the distance between 2D and 3D, a collapse sped by the subsequent intermingling of live-action (Davy Crockett) and animated (*Alice*) properties. Midway through the episode, a shot of *Cinderella*'s (1950) famous transformation into her sparkling dress crossfades into a shot of Walt presiding over a scale model of Disneyland's castle. He hopes aloud that viewers will "find here a place of knowledge and happiness," then adds, "A very favorite storyteller of ours, Uncle Remus, had another name for it; he called it a laughing place." The episode cuts to James Baskett as Uncle Remus in a segment from *Song of the South*, Disney's most notorious live-action animated experiment up to that point, underlining one kind of blending with another.

Subsequent versions of *Disneyland* double underline this blur of live-action and animated properties (and live action's and animation's properties). The 1970s *Wonderful World of Disney* begins with an animated Tinker Bell sprinkling her pixie dust over a photo-realistic castle, giving way to a psychedelic procession of live-action and animated clips. Stock footage of the 1950 Cinderella dancing with Prince Charming gives way to a live-action mascot Mickey riding Dumbo at one of the parks, then, later, an animatronic Mr. Lincoln—all three shots questioning how far we might extend our sense of animation into real life. Other live-action shots, meanwhile—of a bird in the sky, some synchronized dancers, and "it's a small world's" miniature dolls—all appear in differently colored negative, shaded groovily blue or orange or green, looking not unlike animated cels. Elsewhere, the opening juxtaposes a scene of *Alice in Wonderland*'s playing cards marching in step with *Mary Poppins*'s chimney sweeps stepping in time. We even glimpse an actual live-action animated shot—not from *Poppins* but of *Babes in Toyland*'s (1961) stop-motion soldiers.

Later iterations of *Disneyland* don't simply nod to blending but become blended themselves, far beyond Tinker Bell's initial wink. In *Magical World of Disney*'s late-1980s opening, a 2D Sorcerer Mickey (of *Fantasia* fame) stands atop Epcot's geodesic dome, casting magical bolts toward the newly opened Disney–MGM Studios theme park. The camera follows Mickey's sparks into a building there, where we see *another* animated Mickey, his back to us, sitting in front of an editing station. Mickey's monitor shows clips of Jiminy Cricket, Hayley Mills (doubled in *The Parent Trap*), *Tron*'s computer-generated mainframe, and—finally—*Roger Rabbit*'s famous opening, with Roger walking off his animated set and into live action. A superimposed door begins to close on Roger's exit before he forces his way through it and past the camera.

When we get to the early 1990s' *Wonderful World of Disney*, the camera actually goes further, adopting Mickey's point of view at a live-action desk—an inversion of Fleischer's Ko-Ko shorts. Mickey's animated hands paint the Walt Disney Company logo, the luminous blue castle transforming into a 3D structure before a series of shots from the park, *The Little Mermaid*, and *Peter Pan*. When *Honey, I Shrunk the Kids*' giant bee speeds toward us, Mickey's animated hands clasp over the image on the desk, as if the insect's about to buzz into our world. We get more clips—animated (*Fantasia*), live action (*Mary Poppins*'s chimney sweeps again), and something in between: Donald Duck and the actor John Candy chatting in a scene from *Donald, the Star-Struck Duck* (1986); *Roger Rabbit*'s Baby Herman wailing in his live-action pram; and Elton John duetting with Minnie Mouse—"Don't

Go Breaking My Heart"—in 1988's *Totally Minnie*. The early 1990s' *Wonderful World* frames live-action animated mixing within live-action animated mixing. A 1990 episode of the show, "The Muppets at Walt Disney World," concludes with Kermit meeting a 2D Mickey at the actual Magic Kingdom, yet again conflating one form of animation (puppetry) with another, and one major intellectual property with another, in the already mixed-up theme-park space.

By the time we finally reach the late 1990s' and early 2000s' *Wonderful World of Disney* (the last iteration before the advent of streaming), live action and animation actually cohabitate in Sleeping Beauty's castle, here rendered in realistic CG. Tinker Bell swoops into the castle, over a litter of puppies from Disney's 1996 live-action remake of *101 Dalmatians* lolling in the foyer. Past them, Mowgli—from Disney's live-action 1994 *Jungle Book*—stands on the edge of an animated waterfall. On the other side of that, a 2D Captain Hook battles a 2D Peter Pan in front of a porthole showing a scene from *20,000 Leagues Under the Sea*. A 2D Dumbo flies by, directing our attention to windows, bridges, and balconies within the castle populated by the live-action Mighty Ducks, a 2D Beauty and the Beast, and a CG Buzz Lightyear. Elsewhere, Tim Allen (the voice of Buzz) squeezes down a chimney, with some computer-animated assistance, as *The Santa*

Clause's (1994) Santa Claus. Within the castle's walls, live action and animation (both 2D and 3D) share space, as properties literally cross paths. This opening sequence, like those before it, offers an astonishing and not a little prescient image of the big-screen live-action animated mash-ups to come some twenty years later.

MASH-UPS

A certain theme-park logic pervades *Ready Player One* and *Space Jam: A New Legacy*, both produced by the Disney rival Warner Bros. and both of which prolong and dramatize the IP mash-ups that merely serve as *The Magical World of Disney*'s warm-ups. The former film takes place in the near-distant future of 2045—almost exactly a century after Grinde's article—in a world so ravaged by economic and environmental collapse that most of its citizens defect to the OASIS, a vast virtual realm where, as our protagonist, Wade Watts, explains, you can "do anything," like "surf a fifty-foot monster wave in Hawaii," "ski down the pyramids," or "climb Mount Everest with Batman." We see these scenes—and others—as the camera tracks, impossibly, past planets that look a lot like Disney's lands: a self-constructing Minecraft world, a tennis-ball-shaped planet where a golfer slices a shot off a giant pinball bumper, and an intense hurricane where an airborne duo hang glides past a wooden house that looks very much like Dorothy's. The tracking shot settles, finally, on a way station full of lions, tigers, and bears—you name it; in the OASIS, Wade explains, you can be "tall, beautiful, scary, a different sex, a different species, live action, cartoon—it's all your call." True to his word, we see dozens of generic, World of Warcrafted ogres, mages, and elves mulling about, as well as some more specific figures, too: the Cyclops from Harryhausen's *7th Voyage of Sinbad*, RoboCop (from the 1987 film of the same name), and a 3D version of Looney Tunes' Marvin the Martian. The OASIS represents a hub where live action and animation collapse and collide.

The 3D Marvin reappears in *Space Jam: A New Legacy*—a sequel to the 1996 live-action animated movie that piggybacks on the more freewheeling intertextuality of 2003's *Looney Tunes: Back in Action*, which opens on Warner Bros.' backlot. There, Daffy interrupts a live-action *Batman* shoot, trying to make off with the Batmobile; in the studio's commissary, a 2D Shaggy confronts Matthew Lillard (the actor who portrayed him in the live-action *Scooby Doos*); the cafeteria features a poster for *Hoppin' in the Rain*, a *Singin'* parody starring Bugs, Lola Bunny, and Daffy in the Gene Kelly, Debbie Reynolds, and Donald O'Connor roles. Later in the film, Bugs and Daffy encounter a slew of famous aliens in Area

52, including *Forbidden Planet*'s Robby the Robot and a *Doctor Who* Dalek (both belonged to Warner Bros. at the time), as well as Marvin himself. *A New Legacy*, however, takes such cameos to the next level. In the film's final act, the villainous Al G. Rhythm, ruler of the "Serververse"—a galaxy of planets based on Warner Bros. IP, not unlike some of *Ready Player One*'s—presides over a high-stakes basketball game populated by (we assume) the citizens of those planets: animated icons like the Flintstones, the Scooby gang, and King Kong, as well as live-action characters like Batman, Dorothy, Gandalf, some Slytherin students, and *Game of Thrones*' Drogon. Fred Flintstone and company appear in 3D alongside their live-action compatriots, as do the Looney Tunes themselves, whom Al G. "upgrades" from 2D before the big game; "I look expensive!" Daffy declares. Yet again, live action becomes more animated as animation becomes livelier—just as Warner Bros.' formerly discrete properties become more indistinguishable from one another.

PLUS-PLUS

Ready Player One's hub or *A New Legacy*'s game might've looked stranger were it not for the fact that properties like the Flintstones and Game of Thrones *already* stood shoulder to shoulder, in sometimes baffling fashion, on

HBO Max, the Warner Bros. platform on which *Ready Player One* lived and *A New Legacy* debuted (and home, of course, to all those sidelined characters). On streaming platforms, live-action and animated titles mingled far more indiscriminately than they ever did at Blockbuster—more like they did at Disneyland, perhaps. As Madeleine Hunter avers, platforms like Disney+ and Paramount+ "attempt to transform contemporary media and entertainment brands into immersive storyworlds" (204). Like Disney's immersively themed park spaces (Adventureland, Frontierland, Fantasyland, Tomorrowland, and later lands based on hybrid properties like Avatar and Star Wars), Disney+'s animated homepage looked like spokes poking out from Disneyland's Main Street. Disney+'s hub offered clickable windows into the wonderful worlds of classic Disney, Pixar, Marvel, Star Wars, and National Geographic, each with a respective animated flourish: a firework-silhouetted castle, a vertical stream of Toy Story's cloudy wallpaper, rapid-fire comic book panels, hyper-spaced-out stars, a roiling (live-action) mountainscape. Through those windows, viewers might glimpse strictly animated, strictly live-action, live-action animated, or hybrid titles. My Disney clickthrough yielded rows of "Live Action Movies" (with 2019's photo-realistic but CG *The Lion King* up front); "Made in the '90s" (with the partly live-action, partly

stop-motion *James and the Giant Peach* [1996] up front);
and "Inspired by Disney Parks" (with *Muppets Haunted Mansion* [2021] on offer).

Just as *Disneyland* had dramatized Disneyland's indistinction between live-action and animated content—just as *Ready Player One* and *A New Legacy* did as well—so too did the early 2020s advertising that pushed those platforms in the first place. When ViacomCBS relaunched its CBS All Access streaming service as the more expansive Paramount+ in early 2021, its "Sweet Victory" Super Bowl campaign featured a motley crew of live actors and animated characters scaling Paramount Mountain (the famous peak from the studio's logo). In the first spot, *Survivor* host Jeff Probst, tiki torch in hand, leads a group of "heroes and truth seekers, leaders and intellects," including *Star Trek: Strange New Worlds*' Christopher Pike (Anson Mount), Beavis and Butthead, the *Late Late Show* host James Corden, and Dora the Explorer. In a second spot, Dora announces, "according to my [talking] Map, we can climb this [mountain] together!" The former Pittsburgh Steelers coach Bill Cowher—the NFL had joined CBS All Access's fold a few years before—bristles. "Whoa, hold on. Who made you the leader?" he complains. "Just 'cause you have a 'talking map'? I have a talking clipboard." He lifts said clipboard in front of his lips and pitches his voice high: "Hey everybody, I'm a talking clipboard. Coach Cowher's the best! We should follow him. Woohoo!" Like Eddie Valiant in *Roger Rabbit*, Cowher tries to get animated to win his cohort over. In the next spot, Probst scales Paramount Mountain alongside the *Crank Yankers* puppet Elmer Higgins, *Reno 911!*'s Jim Dangle (Thomas Lennon), and *The Ring*'s glitching CG ghoul Samara. They all converge, at long last, atop the peak—not just Probst, Pike, Beavis, Butthead, Dora, Elmer, and Samara but a digitally re-created Lucille Ball and Desi Arnaz, the computer-animated Paw Patrol, a fleshly Stephen Colbert and Patrick Stewart and RuPaul, and a 2D Leonardo (the Teenage Mutant Ninja Turtle). "Don't you see?" explains Young Sheldon (Iain Armitage). "This is a metaphor for how we're all streaming on Paramount+ now."

Given Paramount+'s and other platforms' setups, however, the spot is less than metaphorical, since those hubs (as discussed) narrow the distance between live action and animation, make it domestic and regular, even more than Dave does when he adopts the CG Alvin. "What are we supposed to do up here?" asks *Jersey Shore*'s Snooki. "We dance," replies Stewart; "Sure, let's make it weirder," agrees Colbert, before pressing a button that reads, "DO NOT TOUCH." A miniature dome pops up from the mountain's peak, unveiling SpongeBob SquarePants, in marching-band regalia, performing "Sweet Victory," the song from which the campaign takes its name. Live-action and cartoon stars align above Paramount Mountain, both more and less literally than they do in the studio's animated logo itself. In what the director David Shane calls the campaign's "demented quadratic equation," the "carbon-based" and animated talent amount to equal variables (Bitette).

Disney+ celebrated its second anniversary, in late 2021, with a comparably bat-shit live-action animated mash-up care of *The Simpsons* (the Mouse House acquired Homer and Co. when it bought Fox). *The Simpsons in Plusaversary* imagines various *Simpsons*-fied live-action characters, along with several Disney animated stalwarts, converging on Moe's Tavern. Inside, we find Lisa remade as a Disney princess, trilling, "So let's all celebrate Disney+, as it reaches year number two, / as long as we have your credit card number, it will automatically renew." The camera swirls past characters from Star Wars, Marvel, and Pixar, and Lisa ends up in a kick line between Mowgli and WALL-E; elsewhere, Winnie the Pooh shares a table with Doctor Strange and Buzz Lightyear arm-wrestles with the Mandalorian. Outside, we briefly spy the party's guest list, handled by a haughty Maleficent; it includes Jeff Goldblum, Dopey, Ant-Man, Aaron Burr and King George III (of *Hamilton* fame), Bluey, Luca, Loki, Thanos, and Lighting McQueen. When Homer insists that he's "a big star on Disney+," Maleficent replies, "Oh, I'm sorry, you don't seem to be one of us," as she glances at an iPad tiled with Disney+'s various hubs: Disney, Pixar, ABC, FX, Marvel, Lucasfilm, Hulu, National Geographic, 20th Century Film (no longer Fox), ESPN. In a synergistic coup, Maleficent's iPad makes the metaphor—or new reality—as obvious as Sheldon does in the Paramount campaign: Animated or live action, it's all streaming, dear.

CONCLUSION

In 2023, Disney released *Once upon a Studio*, a nine-minute short celebrating the company's centennial. The Mouse House was founded in 1923, when the distributor Margaret Winkler asked Walt and his brother to produce more Alice films. Befitting a studio that began in the mixed picture business, the short is both live action and animated. *Once upon a Studio* opens at closing time, with animators clocking out of the actual Roy E. Disney Animation Building in Burbank; a giant replica of Mickey's star-spangled, cerulean hat from *Fantasia*'s (1940) "Sorcerer's Apprentice" segment adorns its entrance or, in this case, exit. In the animators' wake, Mickey and company—a century's worth of 2D and CG Disney characters, over five hundred total—emerge from cels and stills on the wall, assembling to take a commemorative photo outside the building's doors. In a madcap, *Roger Rabbit*–esque mash-up, *Aladdin* (1992) and his simian sidekick, Abu, slide down a staircase as *Wreck-It Ralph*'s (2012) CG sweetie Vanellope rounds a corner in her race car, *Oliver & Company*'s (1988) Dodger riding shotgun, kicking up a plume of real-seeming technicolor smoke. That cloud dissipates to reveal Elliott, aka *Pete's Dragon*, one of several live-action animated icons to alight on the eventual (and remarkable) group shot. There, the *Reluctant Dragon* stands out in the back row as *The Three Caballeros'* titular trio preens just a wingspan away from *Mary Poppins*'s penguin waiters. While Roger Rabbit didn't make the final cut, he's front and center in a black-and-white storyboard that the codirector Dan Abraham posted in advance of the short's debut (it's the thought that counts). Despite this mixed company, the only live-action human who halfway keeps up with the toons in *Once upon a Studio* is Walt himself, whose framed portrait gives pause to Mickey while he's conjuring up the crew. In a startling inversion of Walt's address to the framed Mickey in that very first episode of *Disneyland*, the toon offers an earnest and emotional "Thanks" to his creator. He then shrugs shyly and resolves, "On with the show"; the animated mascot and his cohort careen through the studio's corridors en route to their photo op outside, where *Sleeping Beauty*'s (1959) fairy Flora makes the giant, live-action *Fantasia* hat momentarily pink (her sis Merryweather turns it back to blue).

If Mickey's switcheroo in *Once upon a Studio* glances back to the live-action animated film's mixed-up, mashed-up history, it also looks ahead, to the future of what we might more appropriately call the animated live-action film. That appellation could certainly describe Disney's photo-realistic prequel *Mufasa*, released in December 2024, a year or so after *Once upon a Studio*. The film's uncanny mammals inspired the likes of *Vulture*'s Matt Zoller Seitz to ask, in one representative making-of piece, "What do you call this type of movie, anyway?" Disney's CEO, Bob Iger, offers "live action," in keeping with the studio's spate of 2010s remakes; the producer Adele Romanski suggests "photoreal animation"; and while the animation director Daniel Fotheringham accepts "live-action animation," he prefers "virtual production" (qtd. in Zoller Seitz). *Mufasa*, like *The Lion King* (2019) before it, utilized Unreal Engine, "a 3-D image-creation system" derived from "multiplayer video games" (Zoller Seitz), to build environments in which the director Barry Jenkins and the cinematographer James Laxton could shoot as *if* they were behind a live-action camera on set. Laxton trained on an Unreal VCam, "a virtual camera that translates traditional cinematography into a virtual setting" (Zoller Seitz). While the VCam mimicked how Laxton might operate his camera in the real world, that setting also allowed the cinematographer to "stroll through the virtual environment a step at a time or, with the push of a button, cover 100 meters in one step or even fly" (Zoller Seitz). In *Mufasa*, not only is everything the light touches CG, but so too is the light, and the lens, itself. The animated map precedes the live-action territory.

Once upon a Studio unintentionally nods to this new frontier when, at the short's end, Goofy struggles to take the group photo atop a rickety ladder, dropping the (decidedly old-fashioned) live-action camera and smashing it to bits. Where we're going, maybe we don't need cameras—at least not in the traditional sense. Sure, *Wreck-It Ralph*'s digital carpenter, Fix-It Felix, puts the camera back together, but it's Tinker Bell who fixes and freezes the photo for us in the final shot, with a characteristic sprinkle of pixie dust—unreal, indeed. It's as if the cartoon characters in early shorts like *Alice's Wonderland*, who once waved the on-screen hand of the artist away as they took center stage, have taken over not only the easel, or the frame, but the entire set itself. In *Once upon a Studio*, even that artist's hand is animated: *Frozen*'s (2013) CG Olaf scribbles at an animator's desk from which *Aladdin*'s 2D Genie magically emerges. Animation begets animation, just as in *Mufasa*'s simulated cinematography, which aligns more with Tinker Bell and Merryweather and Flora's high-flying magical tactics than Goofy's fragile live-action camera. Disney's centennial short *imagines* a wholly animated studio or soundstage; Jenkins and Laxton actually shot *Mufasa* on one. Not only is the movie animated, but so is its making.

Curiouser and curiously, several of *Once upon a Studio*'s and *Mufasa*'s contemporaries also imagine animation's not-quite-hostile takeover of live action. Jeff Rowe and Kyler Spears's CG *Teenage Mutant Ninja Turtles: Mutant Mayhem*, released just a month before *Once upon a Studio*, at one point follows its famed quartet as they hang back, incognito, at an open-air movie night in Brooklyn. Even though the Ninja Turtles and the humans watching the movie-within-the-movie are animated, the movie-within-the-movie isn't: it's John Hughes's 1986 live-action comedy *Ferris Bueller's Day Off* (like *Turtles*, a Paramount property: synergistic bliss). As we hear the even strains of Wayne Newton's "Danke Schoen," that movie's parade scene takes up the entire frame; Ferris Bueller (Matthew Broderick) rises to perform his famous lip sync. Rowe and Spears then cut to the Turtles, and we now watch the movie over their silhouetted shoulders and shells. "I wish I had hair like that," says Mikey. "I wish I had hair, period," says Donnie. The Turtles' longing swells alongside Newton's (and Bueller's) belting. "Is this high school, like, in real life?" Leo asks. "Yeah," responds a half-serious Raph, "you go to high school, you can just hijack a parade whenever you want." We watch the Turtles watch the human crowd horsing around before Raph says the quiet part out loud: "Maybe one day everyone will love us like everyone loves Ferris Bueller."

If this scene projects a sense of teenage dejection, it also, in its CG/real-life mix, conveys a more animated anxiety: Maybe the Ninja Turtles pine to be live action. The foursome had previously appeared as full-size, part-animatronic puppets (developed by Jim Henson) in 1990's *Teenage Mutant Ninja Turtles* and its sequels, *Teenage Mutant Ninja Turtles II: The Secret of the Ooze* (1991) and *Teenage Mutant Ninja Turtles III* (1993). *TMNT*, a strictly computer-animated sequel to those films, followed over a decade later, in 2007. The Turtles stuck to the small screen for several years before and after, in 4kids's 2D *Teenage Mutant Ninja Turtles* series (2003–9) and Nickelodeon's computer-animated *Teenage Mutant Ninja Turtles* (2012–17). Midway through the latter show's run, Michael Bay rebooted the Ninja Turtles on the big screen, this time as CG heroes in the ostensibly live-action *Teenage Mutant Ninja Turtles* (2014), a box office smash, and its lesser-performing follow-up *Teenage Mutant Ninja Turtles: Out of the Shadows* (2016). By the time *Mutant Mayhem* dropped, the Turtles had traveled from live action to animation and back again.

By *Mutant Mayhem*'s end, after the gang's pal April broadcasts their good intentions to New York City during a climactic battle, the foursome get what they want: not a hijacked parade, alas, but acceptance—at large and into the local high school, which they can now attend by light of day. They join the human, if not necessarily live-action, world. Audiences received the reanimated Turtles with equal enthusiasm. *Deadline*'s Anthony D'Alessandro details how the film grossed nearly $200 million worldwide, "well ahead" of the previous live-action installment from 2016. D'Alessandro declared the film 2023's fourth "most valuable blockbuster" in return on investment, with the turtles bested, not incidentally, by Illumination's CG *Super Mario Bros. Movie* at number one. The new, animated *Super Mario Bros. Movie*, which leveled up to $1.36 billion worldwide, grossed more on its first day of release than 1993's disastrous live-action *Super Mario Bros.* (starring *Roger Rabbit*'s own Bob Hoskins) made in its entire run. In both *Mutant Mayhem* and *Super Mario Bros.*, it paid to be animated.

Still other 2020s blockbusters winked at animation's burgeoning dominance over live action. *Mutant Mayhem* debuted the same year as *Spider-Man: Across the Spider-Verse* (D'Alessandro's *third* most valuable blockbuster and 2023's sixth highest grossing film worldwide), wherein a live-action Donald Glover, as the Spidey foe Prowler, sits imprisoned in the Spider-Society's CG headquarters. "It's rude to stare," he tells the open-mouthed, animated Miles ("Not your Prowler," Miles's own gal pal, Gwen, explains as they traipse through this multiverse). And months before *Mufasa*, another big cat flick batted at live action.

Like *Mutant Mayhem* and *Marios Bros.* before it, Mark
Dindal's *The Garfield Movie* (the twenty-first highest-
grossing film in 2024) forsook its live-action animated
forbears, 2004's *Garfield* and its 2006 sequel, and went
entirely CG—except for one scene in which the orange
tabby wrestles with his hapless owner, John, for control
of the TV. Garfield wants to watch live-action viral cat
videos on Catflix; John wants to watch something more
romantic (a crudely animated live-action couple moon-
ing over each other on a different channel). Garfield wins,
I think, since cute live-action cats—some hugging dogs,
another riding a Roomba—show up in between the film's
end credits. For the next most recent big-screen examples
of animation framing live action as such, we'd have to go
back to Zemeckis's 2004 *Polar Express*, in which Santa's
elves monitor real-life children via a wall of TVs in *their*
headquarters, or 2002's *Lilo and Stitch*, in which the titular
duo admire an actual photograph of Elvis (in *Once upon a
Studio*, the extraterrestrial Stitch gnaws on Goofy's bro-
ken live-action camera before Lilo intervenes).

Like *Once upon a Studio* and *Mufasa*, these features
imagine a world without live action, or a world in which
live action holds only a minority stake. If the Technicolor
musicals and mythic fantasies of the mid-twentieth-
century pic invited live action to dance or fight side by
side with animation, and the cartoon remakes of the

1990s, 2000s, and 2010s domesticated animation by inviting it inside live-action walls, then the 2020s saw live action and animation switching sides or relocating altogether. In the second decade of the twenty-first century, live action moved under animation's roof. In *Once upon a Studio*, animation effectively evicts live action before also heading to the wonderful world outside. *Mufasa* remakes that outside world, imagining the natural world itself—its unspoiled African plains—as animated. *Mutant Mayhem*'s live-action high school fantasy gives way to the quartet's more animated acceptance. *Spider-Verse* jails live action; *The Garfield Movie* considers it a fleeting distraction or melodramatic dreck, one channel you might flip through.

When Nick Grinde wrote of the "part flesh and part ink talking picture" in 1946, he privileged the first part, speculating on the "addition" or "infiltration" of animation into live action (26). But *Once upon a Studio* and company turn live action into the additive and/or perpetrator; live action butts into animation. A century of the latter dancing ever closer to the former, one sometimes-clumsy step at a time, ends with animation taking the lead or delivering the knockout punch—an inversion worthy of Roger Rabbit's Hollywood suburb, where "up is down" and "down is up" (recalling the film's press kit). In the second decade of the twentieth century, it's an animated world; we just happen to live in it. Forget it, folks. It's Toontown.

ACKNOWLEDGMENTS

Thanks, first and foremost, to MaryAnn Jones, for excusing me while I shifted shape over these past few years. Thanks to my unbelievably generous editor, Nicole Solano, who also excused me a few times over, during the pandemic and after. Thanks to Gwendolyn Audrey Foster and Wheeler Winston Dixon for giving me a shot in the first place. Thanks to the anonymous reviewer, who greatly improved my second shot. Thanks to my dean, Christine Spencer, for supporting this project in every way that she could, not in the least by granting me a semester-long sabbatical to research and write toward its end. Thanks to the folks who aided with that research, including Christine Windheuser, Craig Orr, and Kendall McKinley at the National Museum of American History's Archives Center; Vicki Glantz at the University of Wyoming's American Heritage Center; and Barbara Bunting, Ian Post, and Jen Pulsney at Salisbury University's Nabb Center. Thanks to the students who helped me start thinking about this project in the first place, way back in my fall 2020 animation class: Faraji Bartz, Racquel Bazos,

Willard Brookes, Angelica Burton, Daniel Gellasch, Ziti Parilla, Matt Robertshaw, Kezia Robinson, Stevie Sanchez, Jeremiah Thompson, and Jonny Watford. Thanks to those friends and colleagues who continued the conversation, including Todd Harper, Madeleine Hunter, Stephen "Mike" Kiel, Pete Kunze, Tom Leitch, Steven Leyva, and Rick Pallansch. Many thanks to Gabriel Egan and Eckart Voigts for inviting me to present different parts of this book for whip-smart audiences at De Montfort University and Technische Universität Braunschweig. Thanks to my brilliant friend Grant Shreve for getting me back to (and through) my intro and for a heck of a lot else besides. Thanks to Kyle Stine for some Sito; thanks to Tim Mulligan for some *Cinefantastique*; thanks to Kelly Miller for some last-minute intel on *The Garfield Movie*. Thanks to Tracy Lieb and Jeanne-Michele Vigna for keeping my feet on the ground during this project's home stretch. I owe a huge debt of gratitude to Julie Grossman for encouraging me early on and along the way—and just talking Broadway with me when I needed a break. Thanks to my little sis, Brooke Allard, for sitting through many of these films with me the first time around. And thanks to my mum, Elizabeth Meikle, for leaving AMC on.

FURTHER READING

Alexander, Vincent. "Magical Mash-Ups: A History of Live-Action/Animation Hybrids." *Cartoon Brew*, 20 May 2022. www.cartoonbrew.com/cartoon-study/magical -mash-ups-a-history-of-live-action-animation-hybrids -216680.html.

Bouldin, Joanna. "The Animated and the Actual: Toward a Theory of Animation, Live-Action, and Everyday Life." PhD diss., University of California, Irvine, 2004.

Bruckner, Franziska. "Hybrid Image, Hybrid Montage: Film Analytical Parameters for Live Action/Animation Hybrids." Translated by Birgit Haberpeuntner. *Animation*, vol. 10, no. 1, 2015, pp. 22–41.

Crafton, Donald. *Before Mickey: The Animated Film 1898–1928.* Chicago: University of Chicago Press, 1993.

Curtis, Scott, ed. *Animation.* New Brunswick, NJ: Rutgers University Press, 2019.

Lin, Fabia Ling-Yuan. *Doubling the Duality: A Theoretical and Practical Investigation into Materiality and Embodiment of Meaning in the Integration of Live Action and Animation.* Newcastle upon Tyne, UK: Cambridge Scholars, 2014.

Litten, Frederick. "A Mixed Picture: Drawn Animation/ Live Action Hybrids Worldwide from the 1960s to the

1980s." *Litten.de*, 24 Apr. 2011, www.litten.de/fulltext/
mixedpix.pdf.

Telotte, J. P. *Animating Space: From Mickey to Wall-E*. Lexington: University Press of Kentucky, 2010.

WORKS CITED

Anderson, Ross. *The Making of Roger Rabbit: Pulling a Rabbit Out of a Hat.* Jackson: University Press of Mississippi, 2019.

Ball, Sarah. "Mr. Oscar, Tear Down This Wall! Andrew Stanton on How Animated Films Are Pigeonholed— and How Wall-E Is Every Man." *Newsweek*, 23 Jan. 2009. http://blog.newsweek.com/blogs/popvox/archive/2009/01/23/breaking-out-of-the-box-wall-e-director-andrew-stanton-on-the-oscars-the-blurring-of-the-line-between-animation-and-film-and-writing-strong-female-characters.aspx.

Beck, Jerry. "*Roger Rabbit* CG Test." *Cartoon Brew*, 20 Sept. 2010. www.cartoonbrew.com/cgi/roger-rabbit-cg-test-28194.html.

Bentz, Adam. "Emma Stone Responds to Cruella & Joker Movie Comparisons." *ScreenRant*, 31 Mar. 2021. http://screenrant.com/cruella-joker-movie-comparisons-emma-stone-response/.

Berman, Eliza. "5 Photos That Show How *King Kong* Revolutionized Movie Special Effects." *Time*, 9 Mar. 2017. http://time.com/4696931/king-kong-franchise-special-effects/.

Bitette, Nicole. "How the Paramount+ Super Bowl Campaign Came Together." Paramount, 6 Feb. 2021. www

.paramount.com/news/how-the-paramount-super-bowl
-campaign-came-together.

Brodesser-Akner, Claude. "The Inside Story of How *John Carter* Was Doomed by Its First Trailer." *Vulture*, 12 Mar. 2012. www.vulture.com/2012/03/john-carter-doomed -by-first-trailer.html.

Canby, Vincent. "Angela Lansbury in 'Bedknobs and Broomsticks.'" *New York Times*, 12 Nov. 1971. www .nytimes.com/1971/11/12/archives/angela-lansbury-in -bedknobs-and-broomsticks.html.

Cholodenko, Alan. "*Who Framed Roger Rabbit*, or The Framing of Animation." *The Illusion of Life: Essays on Animation*, edited by Alan Cholodenko, Power, 1992, pp. 209–42.

Clarke, Frederick, and Steven Rubin. "Making *Forbidden Planet*." *Cinefantastique*, vol. 8, nos. 2–3, 1979, pp. 4–87.

Common Sense Media. "Alvin and the Chipmunks." 11 Mar. 2025. www.commonsensemedia.org/movie-reviews/ alvin-and-the-chipmunks.

———. "Yogi Bear." 5 Mar. 2025. www.commonsensemedia .org/movie-reviews/yogi-bear.

Connor, J. D. "Space Ghosts: Cartoons and Talk Shows." *Flow*, 16 Apr. 2013. www.flowjournal.org/2013/04/space -ghosts/.

Crafton, Donald. "Animation Iconography: The 'Hand of the Artist.'" *Quarterly Review of Film Studies*, vol. 4, no. 4, 1979, pp. 409–28.

———. *Shadow of a Mouse: Performance, Belief, and World-Making in Animation*. Berkeley: University of California Press, 2012.

Crowther, Bosley. "'Anchors Aweigh,' Gay Musical Film, with Gene Kelly, Frank Sinatra and Miss Grayson, Opens at Capitol Theatre." *New York Times*, 20 July 1945, 15.

———. "Esther Williams Brings Relief from the Heat in 'Dangerous When Wet' at Music Hall." *New York Times*, 19 June 1953, p. 18.

———. "Spanking Disney: Walt Is Chastised for 'Song of the South.'" *New York Times*, 8 Dec. 1946, 85.

———. "'Three Caballeros,' a Disney Picture, with Actors and Animated Characters, in Debut at Globe Theatre." *New York Times*, 5 Feb. 1945, p. 20.

———. "'The Three Caballeros' Shows Brilliant Technique—but Is It Art?" *New York Time*, 11 Feb. 1945, p. X1.

D'Alessandro, Anthony. "'Teenage Mutant Ninja Turtles: Mutant Mayhem' Shockingly Slays Way to No. 4 in Deadline's 2023 Most Valuable Blockbuster Tournament." *Deadline*, 2 May 2024. www.deadline.com/2024/05/teenage-mutant-ninja-turtles-mutant-mayhem-movie-profits-1235902581/.

Diamond, Jamie. "Animation's Bad Boy Returns, Unrepentant." *New York Times*, 5 July 1992. www.nytimes.com/1992/07/05/movies/film-animation-s-bad-boy-returns-unrepentant.html.

Ebert, Roger. "The Best 10 Movies of 1988." *RogerEbert.com*, 31 Dec. 1988. www.rogerebert.com/roger-ebert/the-best-10-movies-of-1988.

———. "Casper." *RogerEbert.com*, 26 May 1995. www.rogerebert.com/reviews/casper-1995.

Ebert, Roger. "'Polar Express' Rides the Rails Through a Child's Heightened Reality." *RogerEbert.com*, 9 Nov. 2004. www.rogerebert.com/reviews/the-polar-express -2004.

Fantasy/Animation. "Episode 33—The Valley of Gwangi (Jim O'Connolly, 1969) (with Astrid Goldsmith)." 4 Nov. 2019. www.fantasy-animation.org/all-episodes/ episode-33-the-valley-of-gwangi-jim-oconnolly-1969 -with-astrid-goldsmith.

———. "Episode 70—Space Jam (Joe Pytka, 1996) (with Paul Wells)." 29 Mar. 2021. www.fantasy-animation.org/ all-episodes/episode-70-space-jam-joe-pytka-1996-with -paul-wells.

Furniss, Maureen. *Art in Motion: Animation Aesthetics*. New Barnet, UK: John Libbey, 2008.

Grinde, Nick. "Greasepaint, Inkwell & Co." *The Screen Writer*, vol. 2, Sept. 1946, pp. 18–26.

Gross, David. "IF, THE STRANGERS: CHAPTER 1, and BACK TO BLACK Openings | Where We Are Now | May 17 to 19, 2024 Weekend." FranchiseRe, 19 May 2024.

Hess, Earl, and Pratibha Dabholkar. *Gene Kelly: The Making of a Creative Legend*. Lawrence: University Press of Kansas, 2020.

Holliday, Christopher. "'You Are Not Responsible for Their Choices, Elsa': *The Lion King* (2019), *Frozen II* (2019) and the Theatre of Photorealist Achievement." *AnimationStudies 2.0*, 3 Feb. 2020. http://blog.animationstudies .org/?p=3466.

Horwitz, Jane. "The Family Filmgoer: 'The Flintstones': Blarney & Retread." *Washington Post*, 2 June 1994, p. D7.

———. "The Family Filmgoer." *Washington Post*, 12 Nov. 2004, p. 41.

Hunter, Madeleine. "We Are in Convergence: Intergenerational Synergies in Twenty-First-Century Children's Media Franchises." PhD diss., University of Cambridge, 2022.

Hunter, Stephen. "The 'Cool World' Is Flat." *The Sun*, 14 July 1992, p. 6C.

Itzkoff, Dave. "A Day Long Remembered: Superfans React to Disney's Acquisition of 'Star Wars.'" *New York Times*, 31 Oct. 2012. https://archive.nytimes.com/artsbeat.blogs.nytimes.com/2012/10/31/a-day-long-remembered-superfans-react-to-disneys-acquisition-of-star-wars/.

Jackson, Devon. "A Full-Court Press in Special Effects." *New York Times*, 17 Nov. 1996. www.nytimes.com/1996/11/17/movies/a-full-court-press-in-special-effects.html.

James, Caryn. "Friendly and Translucent? He's Back." *New York Times*, 26 May 1995, p. C16.

Korkis, Jim. "The Funeral of Marvin Acme." *Cartoon Research*, 2 Apr. 2020. http://cartoonresearch.com/index.php/the-funeral-of-marvin-acme/.

Lennart, Isobel. *Anchors Aweigh* script. 1945. George Sidney Collection, Archives Center, National Museum of American History, Smithsonian Institution.

Litten, Frederick. "A Mixed Picture: Drawn Animation/Live Action Hybrids Worldwide from the 1960s to the 1980s." *Litten.de*, 24 Apr. 2011, www.litten.de/fulltext/mixedpix.pdf.

Manovich, Lev. "What Is Digital Cinema?" 1995. http://

manovich.net/content/04-projects/009-what-is-digital
-cinema/07_article_1995.pdf.

Maslin, Janet. "When 2 Worlds Collide: The Cartoon vs.
the Human." *New York Times*, 11 July 1992. www.nytimes
.com/1992/07/11/movies/review-film-when-2-worlds
-collide-the-cartoon-vs-the-human.html.

Meikle, Kyle. *Adaptation in the Franchise Era: 2001–16*. London: Bloomsbury Academic, 2019.

Mendlesohn, Farah. *Rhetorics of Fantasy*. Middletown, CT:
Wesleyan University Press, 2008.

Merritt, Russell, and J. B. Kaufman. *Walt in Wonderland: The
Silent Films of Walt Disney*. Baltimore: Johns Hopkins
University Press, 1993.

Morgenstern, Joe. "Film: A Darkness on the Edge of Brooklyn." *Wall Street Journal*, 8 June 1995, p. A11.

NowThis Nerd. "Is Ready Player One the New Roger
Rabbit? | NowThis Nerd." YouTube, 27 Mar. 2018. www
.youtube.com/watch?v=NrNcPLCx6AM.

Persons, Dan. "*Casper*: Amblin Owns Memorial Day with
Another CGI Blast from '50s Animation Past." *Cinefantastique*, vol. 26, no. 4, 1995, pp. 14+.

Prince, Stephen. *Digital Cinema*. New Brunswick, NJ: Rutgers University Press, 2019.

Rehak, Bob. "Ubiquitous Animation, 1990–2016." *Animation*, edited by Scott Curtis, New Brunswick, NJ:
Rutgers University Press, 2019, pp. 154–77.

Rivkin, Allen, Laura Kerr, Harry Kurnitz, and Dane Lussier.
My Dream Is Yours script. 1948. Allen Rivkin Papers,
American Heritage Center, University of Wyoming.

Sito, Tom. *Moving Innovation: A History of Computer Animation*. Cambridge, MA: MIT Press, 2013.

Smoodin, Eric. *Animating Culture: Hollywood Cartoons from the Sound Era*. New Brunswick, NJ: Rutgers University Press, 1993.

Space Jam. "Production Notes." 1996. www.spacejam.com/1996/cmp/jamcentral/prodnotesframes.html.

———. "Tech Notes." 1996. www.spacejam.com/1996/cmp/behind/techframes.html.

Stein, Sonja. "Everything Desirable in Musical Comedy Is in 'Anchors Aweigh.'" *Washington Post*, 15 Sept. 1945, p. 8.

Sterritt, David. "Freeze Frames." *Christian Science Monitor*, 16 July 1992, p. 10.

Taylor, Drew. "Welcome to the Remake Kingdom." *Vulture*, 17 May 2017. www.vulture.com/2017/03/beauty-and-the-beast-disneys-remake-machine.html.

Telotte, J. P. *Animating Space: From Mickey to Wall-E*. Lexington: University Press of Kentucky, 2010.

———. "Disney's Alice Comedies: A Life of Illusion and the Illusion of Life." *Animation*, vol. 5, no. 3, 2010, pp. 331–40.

———. *Disney TV*. Detroit: Wayne State University Press, 2004.

Tippett Studio. "Jurassic Park." 2 Sept. 2017. www.tippett.com/portfolio/jurassic-park/.

T.M.P. "Jack Carson, Eve Arden, Doris Day in Musical at Strand—Jungle Film at Rialto." *New York Times*, 16 Apr. 1949, p. 11.

Touchstone Pictures. *Who Framed Roger Rabbit* press kit. Personal collection.

Universal Pictures. *Casper* press kit. Salisbury University, Nabb Research Center, Salisbury, MD.

Vincent, Mal. "'Casper' May Be Friendly, but He Was a Problem to Film." *Virginian-Pilot*, 23 May 1995, p. E1.

Wells, Paul. "Just Do It, Impossible Is Nothing: Animation and Sports Commercials." *Animation and Advertising*, edited by Malcolm Cook and Kirsten Moana Thompson, London: Palgrave Macmillan, 2019, pp. 179–93.

W.H.D. "Gay Musical." *Wall Street Journal*, 24 July 1945, p. 6.

Williams, Esther, with Digby Diehl. *The Million Dollar Mermaid: An Autobiography*. Boston: Mariner Books, 2000.

Zoller Seitz, Matt. "Moonlight in the Lion's Den." *Vulture*, 5 Dec. 2024. www.vulture.com/article/how-and-why -barry-jenkins-made-mufasa-for-disney.html.

SELECTED FILMOGRAPHY

Fantasmagorie (1908)
Gertie the Dinosaur (1914)
The Clown's Pup (1919)
Alice's Wonderland (1923)
Trip to Mars (1924)
Babes in Toyland/March of the Wooden Soldiers (1934)
Hollywood Party (1934)
You Ought to Be in Pictures (1940)
The Reluctant Dragon (1941)
The Three Caballeros (1944)
Anchors Aweigh (1945)
Song of the South (1946)
Fun and Fancy Free (1947)
Mighty Joe Young (1949)
My Dream Is Yours (1949)
The Beast from 20,000 Fathoms (1953)
Dangerous When Wet (1953)
It Came from Beneath the Sea (1955)
Invitation to the Dance (1956)
20 Million Miles to Earth (1957)
The 7th Voyage of Sinbad (1958)
Journey to the Beginning of Time (1960)
Jack the Giant Killer (1962)

The Incredible Mr. Limpet (1964)

Mary Poppins (1964)

Jack and the Beanstalk (1967)

The Valley of Gwangi (1969)

Bedknobs and Broomsticks (1971)

Pete's Dragon (1977)

Clash of the Titans (1980)

Who Framed Roger Rabbit (1988)

"Opposites Attract" (1989)

Jurassic Park (1993)

The Flintstones (1994)

Casper (1995)

Space Jam (1996)

Star Wars: Episode One—The Phantom Menace (1999)

The Adventures of Rocky & Bullwinkle (2000)

The Flintstones in Viva Rock Vegas (2000)

Harry Potter and the Sorcerer's Stone (2001)

The Lord of the Rings: The Fellowship of the Ring (2001)

Scooby-Doo (2002)

Looney Tunes: Back in Action (2003)

Garfield (2004)

Scooby-Doo 2: Monsters Unleashed (2004)

Garfield: A Tale of Two Kitties (2006)

Alvin and the Chipmunks (2007)

Enchanted (2007)

Iron Man (2008)

Alvin and the Chipmunks: The Squeakquel (2009)

Alice in Wonderland (2010)

Yogi Bear (2010)

Alvin and the Chipmunks: Chipwrecked (2011)

The Smurfs (2011)

The Smurfs 2 (2013)

Alvin and the Chipmunks: The Road Chip (2015)

Woody Woodpecker (2017)

Avengers: Infinity War (2018)

Ready Player One (2018)

Avengers: Endgame (2019)

Space Jam: A New Legacy (2021)

Tom and Jerry (2021)

Chip 'n Dale: Rescue Rangers (2022)

Pinocchio (2022)

Once upon a Studio (2023)

Spider-Man: Across the Spider-Verse (2023)

Teenage Mutant Ninja Turtles: Mutant Mayhem (2023)

The Garfield Movie (2024)

How to Train Your Dragon (2025)

INDEX

ABOUT THE AUTHOR

Kyle Meikle is an associate professor of English and communication at the University of Baltimore. He is the author of *Adaptations in the Franchise Era: 2001–16*.